GOODSON MUMBA

Digital Boardroom

Navigating Corporate Governance in the 21st Century

Copyright © 2024 by Goodson Mumba

All rights reserved. No part of this publication may be reproduced, stored or transmitted in any form or by any means, electronic, mechanical, photocopying, recording, scanning, or otherwise without written permission from the publisher. It is illegal to copy this book, post it to a website, or distribute it by any other means without permission.

First edition

ISBN: 9798335777681

This book was professionally typeset on Reedsy. Find out more at reedsy.com

Contents

Preface   v
Acknowledgments   viii
Dedication   ix
Disclaimer   x

1. Chapter One: Introduction to Digital Age Governance   1
2. Chapter Two: Board Dynamics and Digital Leadership   12
3. Chapter Three: Cyber security and Data Privacy Governance   25
4. Chapter Four: Digital Ethics and Corporate Responsibility   39
5. Chapter Five: Innovative Governance Structures and Practices   54
6. Chapter Six: Digital Transformation Strategy and Oversight   69
7. Chapter Seven: E-Governance and Shareholder Engagement   84
8. Chapter Eight: Digital Governance in Mergers and...   98
9. Chapter Nine: Digital Boardroom Tools and Technologies   113
10. Chapter Ten: Governance in the Era of Artificial...   126

- 11 Chapter Eleven: Digital Risk Management and Compliance — 140
- 12 Chapter Twelve: Global Governance in a Digitalized World — 155
- 13 Chapter Thirteen; Environmental, Social, and Governance... — 171
- 14 Chapter Fourteen: Digital Governance and Corporate... — 186
- 15 Chapter Fifteen: Future Trends and Challenges in Digital... — 200
- *About the Author* — 214

Preface

Welcome to "Digital Boardroom Revolution: Navigating Corporate Governance in the 21st Century." This book is a reflection of the profound changes that digitalization has brought to the corporate world, fundamentally altering the landscape of governance.

As we navigate the complexities of the 21st century, the role of corporate boards has evolved significantly. No longer confined to traditional oversight functions, today's boards must grapple with rapid technological advancements, shifting regulatory landscapes, and heightened expectations from a diverse set of stakeholders. These changes demand a new approach to governance—one that is agile, forward-thinking, and deeply integrated with digital capabilities.

In writing this book, we aim to provide a comprehensive guide for board members, executives, and governance professionals who are striving to lead their organizations through this transformative period. We delve into the critical areas that modern boards must master, from understanding the impacts of digitalization on business operations to implementing robust cybersecurity measures, from fostering a culture of innovation to ensuring compliance with complex regulatory requirements.

Each chapter offers a blend of theoretical insights and practical advice, supported by real-world case studies from leading companies that have successfully navigated the digital revolution. Through these examples, we explore how innovative governance structures and practices can drive organizational resilience and sustained success.

Key themes addressed in this book include:

- **The Evolution of Corporate Governance:** Tracing the historical shifts and understanding the current landscape influenced by digital transformation.
- **Digital Risk Management and Compliance:** Strategies for identifying, assessing, and managing digital risks while ensuring regulatory compliance.
- **Cybersecurity and Data Privacy:** Best practices for protecting organizational assets in an era of increasing cyber threats.
- **Innovative Governance Practices:** Exploring the role of technologies like AI, blockchain, and big data in modern governance frameworks.
- **Ethical and Corporate Responsibility:** Balancing profitability with social responsibility and ethical considerations in the digital age.
- **Future Trends in Digital Governance:** Anticipating technological disruptions and preparing for future governance challenges.

Our goal is to equip you with the knowledge and tools necessary to lead with confidence and integrity in the digital era. By embracing the principles and strategies outlined in this book, you can transform your boardroom into a dynamic, innovative, and resilient entity that is well-prepared for the challenges and opportunities of the future.

We invite you to embark on this journey with us, as we explore the digital boardroom revolution and redefine corporate governance for the 21st century.

Sincerely,

Goodson Mumba

Acknowledgments

I wish to express my eternal gratitude to the Almighty God for the boundless wisdom emanating from His universal consciousness, which enriches our understanding of the world. I also extend my heartfelt appreciation to all those who have contributed to my life's journey, providing spiritual, moral, emotional, and material support.

Dedication

I extend my sincerest gratitude to my beloved wife, Edith Mumba, and our children, Angelina, Lubuto, Letticia, Lulumbi, and Butusho, for their unwavering support and understanding throughout the conception, writing, and eventual publication of this book, despite the sacrifices and challenges they endured.

Disclaimer

I extend my sincerest gratitude to my beloved wife, Edith Mumba, and our children, Angelina, Lubuto, Letticia, Lulumbi, and Butusho, for their unwavering support and understanding throughout the conception, writing, and eventual publication of this book, despite the sacrifices and challenges they endured.

1

Chapter One: Introduction to Digital Age Governance

The boardroom of GlobalTech Enterprises buzzed with tension as CEO Emma Carter prepared to address her directors. As she took her seat at the head of the table, she felt the weight of the pivotal moment they were facing.

"Good morning, everyone," Emma began, her voice steady despite the underlying turmoil. "Thank you for joining me today. As you know, we're at a critical juncture in our company's history. The digital revolution is upon us, and we must adapt our governance practices to thrive in this new era."

James Thompson, a seasoned director known for his skepticism towards change, raised an eyebrow. "Emma, are you suggesting we abandon the principles that have served us well for decades?"

Emma met James's gaze, her determination unwavering. "Not abandon, James, but evolve. We can't afford to be left behind while the world embraces digital transformation. Our competitors are already leveraging technology to gain a competitive edge."

Sarah Chen, a younger director with a passion for innovation, nodded in agreement. "Emma's right. We need to embrace technology, not fear it. Digital governance isn't just about compliance; it's about staying agile, transparent, and ahead of the curve."

Emma smiled gratefully at Sarah's support before continuing. "Today marks the beginning of our journey into the world of digital governance. We'll explore the impact of technology on our industry, the challenges we'll face, and the opportunities that lie ahead."

Over the course of the meeting, Emma guided her directors through presentations, case studies, and interactive discussions. They explored the potential of AI-driven analytics to enhance decision-making, the security implications of blockchain technology, and the importance of data privacy in an increasingly connected world.

As the meeting drew to a close, Emma could sense a shift in the room. Skepticism was replaced by curiosity, resistance by openness to change. James, though still cautious, acknowledged the need for adaptation. "You've given us a lot to think about, Emma," he admitted. "Perhaps it's time for us to embrace the digital revolution instead of fearing it."

With a sense of optimism, Emma adjourned the meeting, knowing that the journey ahead would be challenging but necessary. The digital boardroom revolution had begun, and GlobalTech Enterprises was ready to navigate the complexities of corporate governance in the 21st century.

CHAPTER ONE: INTRODUCTION TO DIGITAL AGE GOVERNANCE

Understanding the Evolution of Corporate Governance

After the initial meeting adjourned, Emma scheduled a follow-up session focused on understanding the evolution of corporate governance. She knew that grasping the historical context would be crucial for her directors to fully appreciate the need for adaptation.

As the directors gathered once again in the boardroom, Emma opened the session with a brief history lesson. She traced the origins of corporate governance back to the early industrial era when businesses began to organize themselves into formal structures with boards of directors.

"We've come a long way since then," Emma explained, gesturing to a timeline projected on the wall. "Corporate governance has evolved in response to changing societal norms, economic pressures, and regulatory environments."

She guided her directors through key milestones in governance history, from the rise of shareholder activism in the 20th century to the corporate scandals that shook public trust in the early 2000s. "Each of these events has shaped the way we govern our companies," Emma emphasized.

James leaned forward, his interest piqued. "So, you're saying that corporate governance isn't static? It's constantly evolving to meet new challenges?"

Emma nodded. "Exactly. And right now, we're facing one of the most significant challenges yet—the digital revolution. Technology has fundamentally changed the way we do business, and our governance practices must adapt accordingly."

She proceeded to highlight examples of companies that had successfully embraced digital governance, showcasing their innovative approaches to board composition, decision-making processes, and stakeholder engagement.

As the session drew to a close, Emma encouraged her directors to reflect on the lessons learned. "The past informs the present, but it's up to us to shape the future of corporate governance," she declared. "Let's embrace this opportunity to lead with courage, creativity, and a commitment to excellence."

With newfound clarity and determination, the directors left the boardroom, energized by the prospect of navigating the digital age together. The evolution of corporate governance was underway, and GlobalTech Enterprises was ready to embrace the challenge head-on.

Impact of Digitalization on Business Landscape

As the directors settled into their seats for the next phase of their journey into digital governance, Emma wasted no time in delving into the impact of digitalization on the business landscape. She knew that understanding this crucial aspect was essential for her team to grasp the urgency of their mission.

"Welcome back, everyone," Emma began, projecting a series of charts and graphs onto the screen. "Today, we're going to explore how digitalization is reshaping the very fabric of the business world."

She led her directors through a comprehensive analysis of industry trends, highlighting the exponential growth of technology-driven companies and the disruptive innovations that were revolutionizing traditional markets.

"From artificial intelligence to the Internet of Things, digital technologies are transforming every aspect of our lives," Emma explained. "And as a tech conglomerate, we're uniquely positioned to capitalize on these opportunities—but only if we're willing to adapt."

James frowned, his skepticism evident. "But what about the risks? With great technological power comes great responsibility, as they say. How do we ensure that we're not compromising on ethics or integrity in pursuit of innovation?"

Emma nodded thoughtfully. "That's precisely why we're here today, James. Digital governance isn't just about leveraging technology; it's about doing so responsibly and ethically. We must strike a balance between innovation and integrity, embracing the benefits of digitalization while mitigating the risks."

She proceeded to outline the potential benefits of digitalization for GlobalTech Enterprises, from enhanced productivity and efficiency to greater customer engagement and market agility. But she also emphasized the importance of addressing concerns such as data privacy, cybersecurity threats, and ethical considerations.

"We can't afford to bury our heads in the sand and ignore the realities of the digital age," Emma declared. "The business landscape is evolving whether we like it or not. It's up to us to adapt, innovate, and lead the way forward."

Challenges and Opportunities in the Digital Era

With the stage set and the directors engaged, Emma embarked on the next phase of their exploration: the challenges and opportunities in the digital era. She knew that navigating this landscape would require a careful balance of foresight and adaptability.

"Let's talk about the challenges and opportunities that lie ahead," Emma began, her voice commanding attention as she addressed the room. "The digital era presents us with both unprecedented possibilities and formidable obstacles."

She guided her directors through a comprehensive analysis of the challenges they would face, from the rapid pace of technological change to the complexities of regulatory compliance in a globalized world.

"Adapting to new technologies requires significant investment and resources," Emma explained, her gaze sweeping across the room. "We'll need to stay ahead of the curve, continuously innovating and evolving our strategies to remain competitive."

James furrowed his brow, voicing a concern that echoed in the minds of many. "But what about the risks? With new technologies come new vulnerabilities. How do we ensure the security and integrity of our operations in the face of cyber threats and data breaches?"

Emma nodded in agreement, acknowledging the gravity of James's question. "Cybersecurity is indeed a critical concern," she affirmed. "But it's also an opportunity for us to strengthen our defenses, leverage cutting-edge technologies, and build trust with our customers and stakeholders."

She then pivoted to the opportunities that awaited GlobalTech Enterprises in the digital era, from expanding into new markets and diversifying revenue streams to enhancing customer experiences and driving innovation.

"We have the chance to redefine what it means to be a leader in our industry," Emma declared, her eyes alight with determination. "But it will require courage, creativity, and a willingness to embrace change."

CHAPTER ONE: INTRODUCTION TO DIGITAL AGE GOVERNANCE

Importance of Agile Governance Structures

As the discussion progressed, Emma turned her attention to the importance of agile governance structures in navigating the complexities of the digital era. She knew that in order to thrive in an environment characterized by rapid change and uncertainty, GlobalTech Enterprises would need to adopt a flexible and responsive approach to governance.

"Agility is the key to success in the digital age," Emma began, her voice resonating with conviction. "We must be able to pivot quickly, adapt to changing circumstances, and seize opportunities as they arise."

She guided her directors through the principles of agile governance, emphasizing the need for decentralized decision-making, cross-functional collaboration, and iterative processes.

"Traditional governance structures are often rigid and hierarchical," Emma explained, gesturing towards a diagram of a traditional organizational chart. "But in today's fast-paced environment, we need to empower our teams to make decisions autonomously and respond swiftly to market dynamics."

Sarah nodded in agreement, her enthusiasm evident. "By breaking down silos and fostering a culture of collaboration, we can unleash the full potential of our organization and drive innovation at every level."

James, ever the pragmatist, raised a skeptical eyebrow. "But how do we ensure accountability and oversight in an agile environment? Won't decentralization lead to chaos and inefficiency?"

Emma smiled reassuringly, recognizing the validity of James's concerns. "Agility doesn't mean sacrificing control," she explained. "It means creating clear objectives, establishing transparent metrics for success, and empowering our teams to achieve their goals autonomously."

She then outlined strategies for implementing agile governance structures, from cross-functional task forces and dynamic decision-making frameworks to continuous feedback loops and regular performance reviews.

"As leaders, it's our responsibility to foster a culture of agility and adaptability," Emma declared, her gaze sweeping across the room. "By embracing agile governance, we can unlock new levels of innovation, resilience, and growth."

Overview of Regulatory Frameworks in the Digital Age

With the stage set for their journey into digital governance, Emma turned her attention to the critical topic of regulatory frameworks in the digital age. She knew that navigating the complex landscape of laws and regulations would be essential for GlobalTech Enterprises to operate ethically and responsibly in the digital era.

"Regulatory compliance is non-negotiable," Emma began, her tone firm as she addressed her directors. "As we embrace digital transformation, we must ensure that we adhere to all relevant laws and regulations to protect our company and our stakeholders."

She guided her team through an overview of key regulatory frameworks, from data privacy regulations such as GDPR and CCPA to cybersecurity standards like ISO 27001 and NIST Cybersecurity Framework.

"These regulations are designed to safeguard consumer rights, protect sensitive data, and mitigate cyber threats,"

Emma explained, her voice echoing with authority. "But they also present challenges in terms of compliance, enforcement, and international harmonization."

James, ever the skeptic, raised a skeptical eyebrow. "But won't regulatory compliance stifle innovation and impede our ability to compete in the global marketplace?"

Emma shook her head, dispelling the notion. "On the contrary, James. Regulatory compliance is not a hindrance; it's an opportunity. By proactively adhering to regulations, we can build trust with our customers, enhance our reputation, and gain a competitive advantage in the market."

She then outlined strategies for managing regulatory compliance effectively, from conducting thorough risk assessments and implementing robust compliance programs to fostering a culture of ethics and integrity throughout the organization.

"As leaders, it's our responsibility to ensure that our company operates with the highest standards of compliance and ethics," Emma declared, her voice resolute. "By embracing regulatory frameworks in the digital age, we can build a foundation of trust and accountability that will sustain us through the challenges ahead."

Case Studies: Successful Digital Governance Models

As the directors leaned forward, eager to learn from real-world examples, Emma shifted their focus to case studies of successful digital governance models. She knew that seeing practical applications would inspire her team and provide valuable insights for their own journey.

"Let's take a look at some companies that have successfully embraced digital governance," Emma began, her voice brimming with enthusiasm. "These organizations serve as shining examples of innovation, resilience, and forward-thinking leadership."

She guided her directors through a series of case studies, starting with Alphabet Inc., the parent company of Google. "Alphabet's commitment to transparency and accountability has set the standard for digital governance," Emma explained, highlighting the company's decentralized structure, robust data privacy measures, and proactive approach to cybersecurity.

Next, she turned their attention to Microsoft Corporation, praising the company's agile governance practices and commitment to ethical AI development. "Microsoft's focus on responsible innovation has earned them widespread acclaim and positioned them as leaders in the digital landscape," Emma declared.

As the directors absorbed the lessons from these industry giants, Emma pivoted to a smaller, but equally inspiring, example: Shopify Inc. "Shopify's nimble governance structure and customer-centric approach have propelled them to unprecedented success in the e-commerce space," she explained, citing their innovative use of AI-powered analytics and commitment to data transparency.

Finally, Emma concluded with a case study closer to home: Adobe Inc. "Adobe's transformation from a software company to a digital experience leader is a testament to the power of visionary leadership and strategic adaptation," she declared, highlighting their customer-focused culture, investment in digital innovation, and commitment to corporate social responsibility.

As the directors reflected on these case studies, Emma could sense a shift in the room. The examples of successful digital governance models had sparked inspiration and ignited a sense of possibility among her team.

"These companies prove that digital governance isn't just a buzzword—it's a strategic imperative," Emma declared, her voice echoing with conviction. "Let's learn from their successes and apply these lessons to our own journey forward."

With renewed determination and a wealth of insights to guide them, the directors left the meeting, energized by the prospect of leveraging digital governance to drive GlobalTech Enterprises to new heights of success in the digital age

2

Chapter Two: Board Dynamics and Digital Leadership

Charting a New Course for Leadership

In the sleek boardroom of GlobalTech Enterprises, CEO Emma Carter stood at the head of the table, ready to embark on a crucial discussion about board dynamics and digital leadership. Around her, the directors, a diverse mix of seasoned veterans and fresh-faced innovators, awaited her guidance.

"Good morning, everyone," Emma began, her voice commanding attention. "Today, we're diving into the heart of our digital transformation: the role of the board in shaping our company's future."

She outlined the importance of digital leadership, emphasizing the need for a board that was not only knowledgeable about technology but also willing to embrace change and innovation.

"Our board must be a driving force for digital transformation," Emma declared, her eyes sweeping across the room. "We need leaders who are willing to challenge the status quo, think outside the box, and champion new ideas."

As she spoke, Emma could sense the tension in the room. Some directors, like James Thompson, seemed wary of the unfamiliar territory they were entering. Others, like Sarah Chen, leaned forward with eager anticipation, eager to embrace the challenges ahead.

"To lead in the digital age, we must be agile, adaptable, and forward-thinking," Emma continued, her voice unwavering. "Our board must reflect these values and embody the spirit of innovation that will drive our company forward."

She then turned the discussion to board composition, urging her directors to consider the importance of diversity and inclusion in shaping their leadership team.

"Diverse perspectives lead to better decisions," Emma explained, her passion evident. "We need a board that reflects the diverse world we live in—a board that brings together people from different backgrounds, experiences, and skill sets."

James frowned, his skepticism evident. "But won't too much diversity lead to conflict and discord?"

Emma shook her head, dispelling the notion. "On the contrary, James. Diversity fosters creativity, resilience, and empathy. It allows us to see problems from multiple angles and find innovative solutions that we might not have considered otherwise."

As the discussion unfolded, Emma could feel the energy in the room shifting. The directors, once hesitant and apprehensive, were now engaged and enthusiastic, eager to embrace the challenges and opportunities of digital leadership.

"Leading in the digital age won't be easy," Emma acknowledged, her voice ringing with determination. "But together, as a board, we can chart a new course for GlobalTech Enterprises—one that embraces change, fosters innovation, and paves the way for a brighter future."

With renewed purpose and a shared vision for the road ahead, the directors left the boardroom, ready to embrace their roles as digital leaders and guide GlobalTech Enterprises to new heights of success in the digital age.

Role of the Board in Digital Transformation

As the directors settled back into their seats, Emma turned their attention to the critical role of the board in driving digital transformation. She knew that their leadership would be instrumental in guiding GlobalTech Enterprises through the challenges and opportunities of the digital age.

"The board plays a pivotal role in shaping our company's digital future," Emma began, her voice resonating with authority. "As leaders, it's our responsibility to set the strategic direction, provide oversight, and ensure that our organization remains agile and adaptable in the face of rapid change."

She guided her directors through a comprehensive analysis of the board's responsibilities in digital transformation, emphasizing the need for strategic vision, proactive risk management, and stakeholder engagement.

"Our board must be forward-thinking and visionary," Emma declared, her eyes alight with passion. "We need leaders who can anticipate emerging trends, identify new opportunities, and position our company for long-term success."

James, ever the pragmatist, raised a skeptical eyebrow. "But how do we ensure that our digital initiatives align with our core business objectives?"

CHAPTER TWO: BOARD DYNAMICS AND DIGITAL LEADERSHIP

Emma nodded, acknowledging the validity of James's question. "Alignment is crucial," she affirmed. "That's why our board must work closely with management to develop a clear digital strategy that aligns with our overall business goals and objectives."

She then outlined the board's role in overseeing digital initiatives, from setting performance metrics and monitoring key milestones to evaluating the effectiveness of digital investments and ensuring compliance with regulatory requirements.

"As leaders, it's our responsibility to ask the tough questions, challenge assumptions, and hold management accountable for results," Emma declared, her voice ringing with conviction. "But it's also our responsibility to provide support, guidance, and encouragement as we navigate the complexities of digital transformation together."

As the discussion unfolded, Emma could sense a shift in the room. The directors, once apprehensive about their role in digital transformation, were now engaged and empowered, ready to embrace their responsibilities and lead GlobalTech Enterprises into a new era of digital excellence.

"Digital transformation won't happen overnight," Emma acknowledged, her voice infused with optimism. "But with the dedication, commitment, and leadership of our board, I have no doubt that we can achieve our goals and unlock new opportunities for success in the digital age."

With renewed purpose and a shared commitment to excellence, the directors left the boardroom, ready to embrace their roles as digital leaders and guide GlobalTech Enterprises on its journey of transformation and growth.

Composition of Digital-Ready Boards

As the discussion progressed, Emma shifted the focus to the composition of digital-ready boards, recognizing that the right blend of skills and expertise would be crucial for navigating the complexities of the digital age.

"The composition of our board is key to our success in the digital era," Emma began, her voice carrying a sense of urgency. "We need a diverse and dynamic team of leaders who bring a wide range of perspectives, experiences, and skills to the table."

She guided her directors through the qualities that would define a digital-ready board, emphasizing the importance of technological literacy, industry expertise, and strategic vision.

"We need directors who are not just familiar with technology, but who are passionate about it," Emma explained, her eyes alight with conviction. "We need leaders who understand the potential of digital innovation to transform our business and drive growth."

As she spoke, Emma could see the directors nodding in agreement, their expressions thoughtful and engaged. They understood the importance of assembling a board that was not only capable of guiding GlobalTech Enterprises through the challenges of the digital age but also capable of leading by example.

"We also need diversity in our boardroom," Emma continued, her voice unwavering. "We need diversity of thought, background, and experience. We need leaders who can challenge the status quo, ask the tough questions, and bring fresh perspectives to the table."

James, ever the pragmatist, raised a skeptical eyebrow. "But won't too much diversity lead to conflict and discord?"

Emma shook her head, dispelling the notion. "On the contrary, James. Diversity is our strength. It fosters creativity, innovation, and resilience. It allows us to see problems from multiple angles and find innovative solutions that we might not have considered otherwise."

As the discussion unfolded, Emma could sense a shift in the room. The directors, once hesitant about the idea of diversity, were now embracing it with enthusiasm, recognizing its potential to drive success in the digital era.

"As leaders, it's our responsibility to ensure that our board reflects the diverse world we live in," Emma declared, her voice ringing with conviction. "By assembling a digital-ready board that is diverse, dynamic, and forward-thinking, we can position GlobalTech Enterprises for success in the digital age."

With renewed purpose and a shared commitment to excellence, the directors left the boardroom, ready to embark on the journey of assembling a digital-ready board that would lead GlobalTech Enterprises into a future defined by innovation, growth, and success.

Composition of Digital Literacy among Board Members

As the discussion continued, Emma shifted the focus to the importance of digital literacy among board members, recognizing that a deep understanding of technology would be essential for navigating the complexities of the digital age.

"Our board must be digitally literate," Emma began, her voice carrying a sense of urgency. "We need leaders who not only understand the potential of digital innovation but who are also fluent in the language of technology."

She guided her directors through the qualities that would

define a digitally literate board, emphasizing the importance of staying abreast of emerging technologies, understanding their implications for the business, and leveraging them to drive growth and innovation.

"We can't afford to be bystanders in the digital revolution," Emma explained, her eyes alight with passion. "We need to be active participants, shaping the direction of our company and driving change from within."

As she spoke, Emma could see the directors nodding in agreement, their expressions thoughtful and engaged. They understood the importance of embracing digital literacy as a core competency for effective leadership in the digital era.

"We need to invest in ongoing education and training for our board members," Emma continued, her voice unwavering. "We need to provide them with the tools, resources, and support they need to stay ahead of the curve and make informed decisions about technology."

James, ever the pragmatist, raised a skeptical eyebrow. "But won't it be challenging to ensure that all board members are digitally literate?"

Emma nodded, acknowledging the validity of James's concern. "It won't be easy, but it's essential," she affirmed. "We need to lead by example, demonstrating our commitment to digital literacy and creating a culture of continuous learning and development within our boardroom."

As the discussion unfolded, Emma could sense a shift in the room. The directors, once apprehensive about the idea of digital literacy, were now embracing it with enthusiasm, recognizing its potential to drive success in the digital age.

"As leaders, it's our responsibility to ensure that our board is digitally literate," Emma declared, her voice ringing with conviction. "By investing in education, training, and development, we can empower our board members to navigate the complexities of the digital age with confidence and expertise."

With renewed purpose and a shared commitment to excellence, the directors left the boardroom, ready to embark on the journey of fostering digital literacy among board members and leading GlobalTech Enterprises into a future defined by innovation, growth, and success.

Fostering Innovation and Risk Management

As the discussion progressed, Emma shifted the focus to the critical role of fostering innovation and effective risk management within the boardroom, recognizing that these would be essential components of navigating the digital age successfully.

"Innovation is the lifeblood of our company," Emma began, her voice filled with passion. "We need a board that fosters a culture of creativity, experimentation, and bold thinking."

She guided her directors through the importance of fostering innovation, emphasizing the need for a supportive environment where ideas are encouraged, failures are viewed as learning opportunities, and success is celebrated.

"We can't afford to play it safe in the digital age," Emma explained, her eyes alight with determination. "We need to be willing to take risks, disrupt the status quo, and push the boundaries of what's possible."

As she spoke, Emma could see the directors nodding in agreement, their expressions reflecting a newfound sense of excitement and possibility. They understood the importance of fostering a culture of innovation as a means of driving growth and staying ahead of the competition.

"But with innovation comes risk," Emma continued, her voice growing more serious. "We need to be proactive in identifying and managing potential risks, whether they're related to technology, cybersecurity, or regulatory compliance."

She then outlined strategies for effective risk management, from conducting thorough risk assessments and implementing robust controls to fostering open communication and transparency within the boardroom.

"We need to be vigilant, agile, and responsive," Emma declared, her voice ringing with conviction. "We can't afford to be caught off guard by emerging threats or unforeseen challenges. We need to be proactive in addressing risks and seizing opportunities as they arise."

As the discussion unfolded, Emma could sense a shift in the room. The directors, once apprehensive about the idea of innovation and risk, were now embracing it with enthusiasm, recognizing its potential to drive success in the digital age.

"As leaders, it's our responsibility to foster a culture of innovation and effective risk management within our boardroom," Emma declared, her voice filled with confidence. "By embracing innovation and managing risks effectively, we can position GlobalTech Enterprises for long-term success in the digital age."

With renewed purpose and a shared commitment to excellence, the directors left the boardroom, ready to embark on the journey of fostering innovation and effective risk management within their organization, and leading GlobalTech Enterprises into a future defined by innovation, growth, and success.

CHAPTER TWO: BOARD DYNAMICS AND DIGITAL LEADERSHIP

Enhancing Board Effectiveness Through Technology

As the discussion continued, Emma directed the attention of the board to the crucial aspect of enhancing board effectiveness through the strategic utilization of technology. She understood that embracing digital tools and platforms would be instrumental in driving efficiency, transparency, and collaboration within the boardroom.

"Leveraging technology is essential for enhancing our board's effectiveness," Emma began, her voice resonating with determination. "We need to embrace digital tools and platforms that streamline processes, facilitate communication, and enable informed decision-making."

She guided her directors through the potential benefits of technology in enhancing board effectiveness, from digital board portals and secure communication platforms to data analytics and AI-driven insights.

"With the right technology in place, we can improve the efficiency of board meetings, ensure timely access to relevant information, and empower directors to make more informed decisions," Emma explained, her eyes alight with excitement.

As she spoke, Emma could see the directors nodding in agreement, their expressions reflecting a growing appreciation for the transformative potential of technology. They understood that by embracing digital tools and platforms, they could elevate the effectiveness and impact of their boardroom discussions and decisions.

"But with technology comes responsibility," Emma continued, her tone growing more serious. "We need to ensure that the digital tools and platforms we adopt are secure, reliable, and compliant with regulatory requirements."

She then outlined strategies for effectively integrating technology into board operations, from conducting thorough due diligence and selecting reputable vendors to providing comprehensive training and support for board members.

"As leaders, it's our responsibility to embrace technology as a means of enhancing board effectiveness," Emma declared, her voice filled with conviction. "By leveraging digital tools and platforms strategically, we can drive efficiency, transparency, and collaboration within our boardroom, and position GlobalTech Enterprises for success in the digital age."

As the discussion unfolded, Emma could sense a palpable excitement in the room. The directors, once apprehensive about the idea of technology, were now embracing it with enthusiasm, recognizing its potential to revolutionize the way they worked and collaborated.

"With the right technology at our disposal, there's no limit to what we can achieve as a board," Emma concluded, her voice ringing with confidence. "Let's embrace this opportunity to enhance our effectiveness and drive GlobalTech Enterprises forward into a future defined by innovation, growth, and success."

Cultivating a Culture of Continuous Learning

As the discussion progressed, Emma turned the attention of the board to the vital aspect of cultivating a culture of continuous learning within the organization. She knew that in order to thrive in the ever-evolving landscape of the digital age, GlobalTech Enterprises would need to prioritize learning, adaptation, and growth at all levels.

"Cultivating a culture of continuous learning is essential

for our success in the digital era," Emma began, her voice filled with conviction. "We need a workforce that is curious, adaptable, and committed to personal and professional development."

She guided her directors through the importance of fostering a culture of continuous learning, emphasizing the need for ongoing education, training, and skill development.

"In the fast-paced world of technology, what we know today may not be enough tomorrow," Emma explained, her eyes shining with passion. "We need to be constantly learning, evolving, and staying ahead of the curve."

As she spoke, Emma could see the directors nodding in agreement, their expressions reflecting a shared commitment to the value of lifelong learning. They understood that by investing in their own development and that of their employees, they could create a culture of innovation, resilience, and growth within GlobalTech Enterprises.

"But cultivating a culture of continuous learning requires more than just providing training opportunities," Emma continued, her tone growing more serious. "It requires leadership, support, and a commitment to fostering a learning mindset at all levels of the organization."

She then outlined strategies for effectively cultivating a culture of continuous learning, from leading by example and promoting knowledge sharing to providing resources, support, and recognition for learning achievements.

"As leaders, it's our responsibility to create an environment where learning is celebrated, encouraged, and embedded into the fabric of our organization," Emma declared, her voice ringing with conviction. "By fostering a culture of continuous learning, we can empower our employees to reach their full potential, adapt to change, and drive innovation at every level."

As the discussion unfolded, Emma could sense a palpable excitement in the room. The directors, once hesitant about the idea of continuous learning, were now embracing it with enthusiasm, recognizing its potential to unlock new opportunities and drive success in the digital age.

"With a culture of continuous learning at our core, there's no limit to what we can achieve as an organization," Emma concluded, her voice filled with optimism. "Let's embrace this opportunity to invest in our greatest asset—our people—and pave the way for a future defined by growth, innovation, and success."

3

Chapter Three: Cyber security and Data Privacy Governance

Navigating Cybersecurity and Data Privacy Governance

In the heart of GlobalTech Enterprises' headquarters, CEO Emma Carter convened the board for a crucial discussion on cybersecurity and data privacy governance. With the digital landscape evolving at breakneck speed, Emma knew that safeguarding the company's assets and protecting sensitive data were paramount to its success in the digital age.

"Welcome, everyone," Emma began, her voice echoing with gravitas as she addressed the assembled directors. "Today, we're delving into the critical realm of cybersecurity and data privacy governance—a topic that is more pressing now than ever before."

She guided her directors through an overview of the cybersecurity landscape, highlighting the growing threat of cyberattacks, data breaches, and malicious actors seeking to exploit vulnerabilities in the digital ecosystem.

"Our company's digital assets are among our most valuable resources," Emma emphasized, her eyes scanning the room. "We must do everything in our power to protect them from harm and ensure the integrity, confidentiality, and availability of our data."

As she spoke, Emma could see the directors nodding in agreement, their expressions reflecting a shared understanding of the importance of cybersecurity in safeguarding the company's interests.

"But cybersecurity isn't just a technology issue—it's a governance issue," Emma continued, her voice growing more serious. "We need robust governance frameworks in place to ensure that our cybersecurity measures are effective, resilient, and aligned with our business objectives."

She then turned the discussion to data privacy, outlining the regulatory landscape and the importance of protecting customer data and respecting privacy rights.

"Our customers trust us with their sensitive information," Emma declared, her tone unwavering. "We have a responsibility to safeguard their privacy, protect their data, and uphold their trust in our brand."

As the discussion unfolded, Emma could sense a palpable tension in the room. The directors, once confident in their understanding of cybersecurity and data privacy, were now grappling with the enormity of the task ahead.

"But with great responsibility comes great opportunity," Emma declared, her voice ringing with conviction. "By prioritizing cybersecurity and data privacy governance, we can not only protect our company from harm but also differentiate ourselves in the marketplace and build trust with our customers and stakeholders."

With renewed purpose and a shared commitment to excellence, the directors left the boardroom, ready to embark on the journey of strengthening cybersecurity and data privacy governance within GlobalTech Enterprises, and leading the company into a future defined by security, trust, and resilience.

Understanding Cybersecurity Risks in the Digital Age

As the discussion continued, Emma shifted the focus to understanding cybersecurity risks in the digital age. She knew that in order to effectively safeguard GlobalTech Enterprises from potential threats, the board needed to have a comprehensive understanding of the evolving landscape of cyber risks.

"The digital age has brought with it unprecedented opportunities, but also unprecedented risks," Emma began, her voice carrying a sense of urgency. "We must be vigilant in our efforts to identify, assess, and mitigate these risks to protect our company's assets and reputation."

She guided her directors through an analysis of the cybersecurity landscape, highlighting the various threats and vulnerabilities that GlobalTech Enterprises could potentially face, from malware and phishing attacks to insider threats and supply chain vulnerabilities.

"Our adversaries are becoming increasingly sophisticated and relentless in their pursuit of our data," Emma explained, her eyes scanning the room. "We need to stay one step ahead of them by understanding their tactics, techniques, and procedures, and by implementing robust cybersecurity measures to defend against them."

As she spoke, Emma could see the directors nodding in agreement, their expressions reflecting a growing awareness of the gravity of the situation. They understood that in the digital age, cybersecurity was not just a technical issue—it was a strategic imperative that required the attention and commitment of the entire organization.

"But understanding cybersecurity risks is just the first step," Emma continued, her voice growing more serious. "We also need to develop a proactive and holistic approach to managing these risks, one that encompasses people, processes, and technology."

She then outlined strategies for effectively managing cybersecurity risks, from conducting regular risk assessments and implementing multi-layered security controls to providing comprehensive training and awareness programs for employees.

"As leaders, it's our responsibility to ensure that cybersecurity is embedded into the fabric of our organization," Emma declared, her tone unwavering. "By prioritizing cybersecurity risk management, we can mitigate threats, protect our assets, and build resilience against future attacks."

As the discussion unfolded, Emma could sense a palpable determination in the room. The directors, once daunted by the complexity of cybersecurity risks, were now embracing the challenge with renewed vigor, recognizing it as an opportunity to strengthen GlobalTech Enterprises' defenses and position the company for long-term success in the digital age.

"With a clear understanding of cybersecurity risks and a proactive approach to managing them, there's no limit to what we can achieve as a company," Emma concluded, her voice filled with confidence. "Let's embrace this opportunity to protect our company, our customers, and our stakeholders, and lead GlobalTech Enterprises into a future defined by security, trust, and resilience."

Establishing Robust Data Protection Policies

As the discussion continued, Emma directed the attention of the board to the critical task of establishing robust data protection policies. She understood that in the digital age, data was not just a valuable asset—it was also a potential liability if not properly protected.

"Our data is one of our most valuable assets," Emma began, her voice filled with gravitas. "But it's also one of our most vulnerable. We must establish robust data protection policies to safeguard our data from unauthorized access, disclosure, or misuse."

She guided her directors through an analysis of the importance of data protection, highlighting the potential consequences of data breaches, including financial loss, reputational damage, and regulatory penalties.

"As custodians of our customers' data, we have a responsibility to protect their privacy and uphold their trust in our brand," Emma declared, her eyes scanning the room. "That begins with establishing clear, comprehensive, and enforceable data protection policies."

As she spoke, Emma could see the directors nodding in agreement, their expressions reflecting a shared commitment to the importance of data protection. They understood that in the digital age, data was both a valuable asset and a potential liability, and that robust policies were essential for safeguarding it.

"But establishing data protection policies is just the first step," Emma continued, her voice growing more serious. "We also need to ensure that these policies are effectively implemented, monitored, and enforced throughout the organization."

She then outlined strategies for effectively establishing data protection policies, from conducting data inventories and risk assessments to implementing access controls and encryption measures.

"As leaders, it's our responsibility to create a culture of data protection within our organization," Emma declared, her tone unwavering. "By prioritizing data protection and embedding it into our day-to-day operations, we can mitigate risks, protect our assets, and build trust with our customers and stakeholders."

As the discussion unfolded, Emma could sense a palpable determination in the room. The directors, once daunted by the complexity of data protection, were now embracing the challenge with renewed vigor, recognizing it as an opportunity to strengthen GlobalTech Enterprises' defenses and position the company for long-term success in the digital age.

"With robust data protection policies in place, we can protect our data, our customers, and our stakeholders, and lead GlobalTech Enterprises into a future defined by security, trust, and resilience," Emma concluded, her voice filled with confidence. "Let's embrace this opportunity to safeguard our most valuable asset and uphold the highest standards of data protection."

Compliance with Data Privacy Regulations <e g., GDPR, CCPA)

As the discussion continued, Emma shifted the focus to the critical task of ensuring compliance with data privacy regulations, such as the GDPR and CCPA. She understood that in the digital age, regulatory compliance was not optional—it was a legal requirement and a fundamental obligation to protect the rights and privacy of individuals.

"Our customers entrust us with their sensitive information, and it's our responsibility to protect their privacy and uphold their rights," Emma began, her voice carrying a sense of urgency. "That means ensuring compliance with data privacy regulations, such as the GDPR and CCPA, which set strict standards for the collection, use, and protection of personal data."

She guided her directors through an analysis of the key provisions of these regulations, highlighting the importance of transparency, accountability, and consent in data processing.

"As a global company, we operate in a complex regulatory landscape, with laws and regulations that vary from region to region," Emma explained, her eyes scanning the room. "But regardless of where we operate, we must comply with the highest standards of data privacy to protect our customers and uphold their trust in our brand."

As she spoke, Emma could see the directors nodding in agreement, their expressions reflecting a growing awareness of the importance of regulatory compliance. They understood that failure to comply with data privacy regulations could not only result in significant financial penalties but also irreparable damage to the company's reputation.

"But compliance with data privacy regulations is not just a legal obligation—it's also an opportunity," Emma continued, her voice growing more serious. "By demonstrating our commitment to data privacy and adopting best practices for compliance, we can differentiate ourselves in the marketplace, build trust with our customers, and drive long-term value for our business."

She then outlined strategies for effectively achieving compliance with data privacy regulations, from conducting data audits and implementing privacy-by-design principles to establishing robust data protection measures and appointing a dedicated data protection officer.

"As leaders, it's our responsibility to ensure that our company complies with data privacy regulations and upholds the highest standards of data protection," Emma declared, her tone unwavering. "By prioritizing compliance and embedding it into our corporate culture, we can protect our customers, mitigate risks, and build trust with our stakeholders."

As the discussion unfolded, Emma could sense a palpable determination in the room. The directors, once daunted by the complexity of data privacy regulations, were now embracing the challenge with renewed vigor, recognizing it as an opportunity to demonstrate leadership, integrity, and commitment to ethical business practices.

"With compliance with data privacy regulations as our guiding principle, we can protect our customers, uphold their trust, and lead GlobalTech Enterprises into a future defined by security, trust, and resilience," Emma concluded, her voice filled with confidence. "Let's embrace this opportunity to demonstrate our commitment to data privacy and set the standard for responsible data management in the digital age."

CHAPTER THREE: CYBER SECURITY AND DATA PRIVACY GOVERNANCE

Cyber Incident Response and Crisis Management

As the discussion progressed, Emma turned the attention of the board to the critical task of cyber incident response and crisis management. She knew that despite the best preventive measures, cyberattacks could still occur, and the company needed to be prepared to respond swiftly and effectively to mitigate the impact.

"Cyber incidents are not a matter of if, but when," Emma began, her voice filled with gravity. "We must be prepared to respond quickly and decisively to any cybersecurity incidents that may occur, to minimize the damage and protect our company's interests."

She guided her directors through an analysis of the importance of cyber incident response and crisis management, highlighting the potential consequences of a cyberattack, including financial loss, reputational damage, and legal liability.

"Our response to a cyber incident can make all the difference in how we weather the storm," Emma explained, her eyes scanning the room. "We need to have clear policies, procedures, and protocols in place to guide our response and ensure that we can recover from an attack as quickly and effectively as possible."

As she spoke, Emma could see the directors nodding in agreement, their expressions reflecting a growing understanding of the importance of preparedness in the face of cyber threats. They understood that a proactive approach to cyber incident response could mean the difference between resilience and ruin.

"But cyber incident response is not just a technical issue—it's also a leadership issue," Emma continued, her voice growing more serious. "We need strong leadership and effective communication to guide our response, coordinate our efforts, and reassure stakeholders during a crisis."

She then outlined strategies for effectively managing cyber incidents and crises, from establishing incident response teams and conducting regular drills to developing communication plans and engaging with stakeholders proactively.

"As leaders, it's our responsibility to ensure that our company is prepared to respond to cyber incidents and crises with speed, agility, and resilience," Emma declared, her tone unwavering. "By prioritizing cyber incident response and crisis management, we can protect our company, our customers, and our stakeholders, and emerge stronger from any adversity we may face."

As the discussion unfolded, Emma could sense a palpable determination in the room. The directors, once daunted by the prospect of cyber incidents, were now embracing the challenge with renewed vigor, recognizing it as an opportunity to demonstrate leadership, resilience, and commitment to protecting GlobalTech Enterprises' interests.

"With a proactive approach to cyber incident response and crisis management, there's no limit to what we can achieve as a company," Emma concluded, her voice filled with confidence. "Let's embrace this opportunity to prepare for the worst, so that we can emerge stronger and more resilient in the face of any cyber threat."

CHAPTER THREE: CYBER SECURITY AND DATA PRIVACY GOVERNANCE

Board Oversight of Cybersecurity Measures

As the discussion continued, Emma directed the attention of the board to the crucial aspect of board oversight of cybersecurity measures. She understood that effective oversight was essential for ensuring that the company's cybersecurity efforts were aligned with its strategic objectives and that adequate resources were allocated to protect against emerging threats.

"The board plays a critical role in overseeing our company's cybersecurity measures," Emma began, her voice filled with authority. "We must ensure that our cybersecurity efforts are robust, proactive, and aligned with our business objectives."

She guided her directors through an analysis of the importance of board oversight of cybersecurity, highlighting the need for clear policies, processes, and reporting mechanisms to monitor and evaluate the effectiveness of cybersecurity measures.

"As directors, we have a fiduciary duty to protect the interests of our company and its stakeholders," Emma explained, her eyes scanning the room. "That includes overseeing our cybersecurity efforts and holding management accountable for maintaining adequate safeguards to protect our assets and data."

As she spoke, Emma could see the directors nodding in agreement, their expressions reflecting a growing understanding of the board's role in cybersecurity oversight. They understood that effective oversight was essential for identifying gaps, assessing risks, and ensuring that the company remained resilient in the face of evolving threats.

"But board oversight of cybersecurity is not just about monitoring—it's also about leadership," Emma continued, her voice growing more serious. "We need to set the tone from the top, prioritize cybersecurity as a strategic imperative, and demonstrate our commitment to protecting our company from cyber threats."

She then outlined strategies for effective board oversight of cybersecurity measures, from establishing cybersecurity committees and conducting regular reviews to engaging with external experts and staying informed about emerging threats and best practices.

"As leaders, it's our responsibility to ensure that our company's cybersecurity efforts are robust, proactive, and aligned with our strategic objectives," Emma declared, her tone unwavering. "By prioritizing board oversight of cybersecurity measures, we can protect our company, our customers, and our stakeholders, and position GlobalTech Enterprises for long-term success in the digital age."

As the discussion unfolded, Emma could sense a palpable determination in the room. The directors, once hesitant about their role in cybersecurity oversight, were now embracing the challenge with renewed vigor, recognizing it as an opportunity to demonstrate leadership, accountability, and commitment to protecting the company's interests.

"With effective board oversight of cybersecurity measures, there's no limit to what we can achieve as a company," Emma concluded, her voice filled with confidence. "Let's embrace this opportunity to prioritize cybersecurity, protect our assets, and lead GlobalTech Enterprises into a future defined by security, resilience, and success."

Investing in Cybersecurity Technologies and Training

As the discussion progressed, Emma shifted the focus to the crucial task of investing in cybersecurity technologies and training. She understood that in the rapidly evolving landscape of cyber threats, staying ahead of the curve required not only cutting-edge technology but also a skilled and knowledgeable workforce.

"As the guardians of GlobalTech Enterprises' digital assets, it's imperative that we invest in the right cybersecurity technologies and provide our employees with the necessary training to defend against evolving threats," Emma began, her voice resonating with authority. "Our cybersecurity posture is only as strong as our weakest link, and it's our responsibility to ensure that we have the tools and expertise to protect our company from harm."

She guided her directors through an analysis of the importance of investing in cybersecurity technologies, highlighting the role of technologies such as firewalls, intrusion detection systems, and encryption in safeguarding against cyber threats.

"Our adversaries are constantly evolving, and so must we," Emma explained, her eyes scanning the room. "We need to invest in technologies that not only detect and prevent cyber-attacks but also enable us to respond quickly and effectively in the event of a breach."

As she spoke, Emma could see the directors nodding in agreement, their expressions reflecting a growing understanding of the importance of technology in cybersecurity defense. They understood that by investing in the right tools and technologies, they could strengthen GlobalTech Enterprises' defenses and mitigate the risk of cyber threats.

"But technology alone is not enough," Emma continued, her voice growing more serious. "We also need to invest in training and development to ensure that our employees have the knowledge and skills to effectively use these technologies and defend against cyber threats."

She then outlined strategies for investing in cybersecurity training, from providing regular awareness programs and simulations to offering specialized courses and certifications for IT professionals.

"As leaders, it's our responsibility to ensure that our employees are equipped with the knowledge and skills they need to defend against cyber threats," Emma declared, her tone unwavering. "By investing in cybersecurity training, we can build a culture of security awareness, resilience, and accountability within our organization, and strengthen our defenses against cyber threats."

As the discussion unfolded, Emma could sense a palpable determination in the room. The directors, once hesitant about the costs and complexities of cybersecurity investments, were now embracing the challenge with renewed vigor, recognizing it as an opportunity to demonstrate leadership, foresight, and commitment to protecting GlobalTech Enterprises' interests.

"With the right investments in cybersecurity technologies and training, there's no limit to what we can achieve as a company," Emma concluded, her voice filled with confidence. "Let's embrace this opportunity to strengthen our defenses, protect our assets, and lead GlobalTech Enterprises into a future defined by security, resilience, and success."

4

Chapter Four: Digital Ethics and Corporate Responsibility

"Guardians of Integrity: Navigating Digital Ethical and Corporate Responsibility"

In the heart of GlobalTech Enterprises' headquarters, CEO Emma Carter convened the board for a crucial discussion on digital ethical and corporate responsibility. With the increasing integration of technology into every aspect of business, Emma knew that upholding ethical standards and corporate responsibility were more critical than ever.

"Welcome, everyone," Emma began, her voice commanding attention as she addressed the assembled directors. "Today, we're delving into the vital realm of digital ethical and corporate responsibility—a topic that is foundational to our company's integrity and reputation."

She guided her directors through an exploration of the importance of ethical behavior and corporate responsibility in the digital age, highlighting the potential consequences of unethical actions, including reputational damage, legal liabilities, and loss of stakeholder trust.

"As leaders of GlobalTech Enterprises, we have a responsibility not only to our shareholders but also to our employees, customers, and the communities in which we operate," Emma explained, her eyes scanning the room. "That responsibility extends to upholding the highest standards of ethical conduct and corporate responsibility in everything we do."

As she spoke, Emma could see the directors nodding in agreement, their expressions reflecting a shared commitment to ethical leadership and corporate citizenship. They understood that in the digital age, ethical lapses could have far-reaching consequences, impacting not only the company's bottom line but also its long-term sustainability and success.

"But upholding ethical standards and corporate responsibility is not just a matter of compliance—it's also about leadership," Emma continued, her voice growing more serious. "We need to set the tone from the top, prioritize ethical behavior and corporate responsibility, and hold ourselves and others accountable for upholding these values."

She then outlined strategies for effectively integrating ethical considerations into business practices, from establishing clear codes of conduct and ethics training programs to implementing mechanisms for reporting and addressing unethical behavior.

"As leaders, it's our responsibility to create a culture of integrity, transparency, and accountability within our organization," Emma declared, her tone unwavering. "By prioritizing digital ethical and corporate responsibility, we can build trust with our stakeholders, enhance our reputation, and create long-term value for our company."

As the discussion unfolded, Emma could sense a palpable determination in the room. The directors, once focused solely on financial performance, were now embracing the broader implications of ethical leadership and corporate responsibility, recognizing them as essential components of sustainable business success.

"With a commitment to digital ethical and corporate responsibility at our core, there's no limit to what we can achieve as a company," Emma concluded, her voice filled with confidence. "Let's embrace this opportunity to lead with integrity, uphold our responsibilities, and inspire trust in GlobalTech Enterprises as a beacon of ethical leadership in the digital age."

Ethical Implications of Digital Technologies

As the discussion continued, Emma directed the focus to the ethical implications of digital technologies. She knew that as GlobalTech Enterprises embraced innovation and pushed the boundaries of technology, it was essential to consider the ethical ramifications of their actions.

"The rapid advancement of digital technologies brings with it a host of ethical considerations that we must address," Emma began, her voice resonating with seriousness. "From artificial intelligence and machine learning to data analytics and automation, every technological innovation we pursue has the potential to impact society in profound ways."

She guided her directors through an exploration of the ethical dilemmas posed by digital technologies, highlighting issues such as privacy infringement, algorithmic bias, and the displacement of workers by automation.

"As leaders in the digital age, we have a responsibility to anticipate and mitigate the ethical risks associated with our technological advancements," Emma explained, her eyes scanning the room. "We cannot afford to prioritize innovation at the expense of ethics. We must ensure that our products and services are designed and deployed in ways that respect human dignity, privacy, and autonomy."

As she spoke, Emma could see the directors nodding in agreement, their expressions reflecting a growing understanding of the complexity of the ethical challenges they faced. They understood that as stewards of technology, they had a duty to consider the broader societal implications of their actions and make decisions that aligned with ethical principles.

"But addressing the ethical implications of digital technologies requires more than just awareness—it requires action," Emma continued, her voice growing more serious. "We need to embed ethical considerations into every stage of the technology development lifecycle, from design and development to deployment and evaluation."

She then outlined strategies for effectively addressing the ethical implications of digital technologies, from conducting ethical impact assessments and engaging with stakeholders to establishing ethical guidelines and governance structures.

"As leaders, it's our responsibility to ensure that our technological advancements are guided by ethical principles and contribute to the greater good," Emma declared, her tone unwavering. "By prioritizing ethics in our decision-making processes, we can build trust with our customers, protect our reputation, and create a more sustainable and equitable future for all."

As the discussion unfolded, Emma could sense a palpable

determination in the room. The directors, once focused solely on technological innovation, were now embracing the ethical imperative of their actions, recognizing it as essential to their role as responsible corporate citizens in the digital age.

"With a commitment to addressing the ethical implications of digital technologies, we can lead by example and inspire positive change in our industry and beyond," Emma concluded, her voice filled with conviction. "Let's embrace this opportunity to shape a future where technology serves humanity and upholds our highest ethical standards."

Integrating Ethics into Corporate Culture

As the discussion continued, Emma shifted the focus to the critical task of integrating ethics into corporate culture. She understood that for ethical principles to guide decision-making at every level of the organization, they needed to be deeply ingrained in the company's values, norms, and behaviors.

"Our corporate culture is the foundation upon which our company stands," Emma began, her voice carrying a sense of urgency. "To truly embed ethics into our organization, we must ensure that ethical considerations are not just an afterthought, but an integral part of how we do business."

She guided her directors through an exploration of the importance of corporate culture in shaping ethical behavior, highlighting the role of leadership, communication, and accountability in fostering a culture of integrity and ethical decision-making.

"As leaders, we have a responsibility to set the tone from the top and lead by example," Emma explained, her eyes scanning the room. "We must demonstrate our commitment to ethics in everything we do, from how we treat our employees and customers to how we engage with our suppliers and partners."

As she spoke, Emma could see the directors nodding in agreement, their expressions reflecting a growing understanding of the pivotal role of corporate culture in promoting ethical behavior. They understood that a strong ethical culture was not only essential for mitigating risks and building trust but also for attracting and retaining top talent.

"But integrating ethics into corporate culture is not just about leadership—it's also about empowerment," Emma continued, her voice growing more serious. "We need to empower our employees to speak up when they see unethical behavior, to challenge the status quo, and to make decisions that align with our values and principles."

She then outlined strategies for effectively integrating ethics into corporate culture, from providing ethics training and resources to promoting open communication and fostering a supportive environment for ethical decision-making.

"As leaders, it's our responsibility to create a culture where ethics are not just a compliance issue, but a way of life," Emma declared, her tone unwavering. "By prioritizing ethics in our corporate culture, we can build trust, enhance our reputation, and create a more resilient and sustainable organization for the future."

As the discussion unfolded, Emma could sense a palpable determination in the room. The directors, once focused solely on financial performance, were now embracing the broader implications of corporate culture, recognizing it as essential to their role as responsible stewards of the company's reputation and success.

"With a commitment to integrating ethics into our corporate culture, we can build a stronger, more resilient organization that upholds the highest standards of integrity and accountability," Emma concluded, her voice filled with confidence. "Let's embrace this opportunity to lead by example and inspire a culture where ethics are not just a part of what we do, but who we are."

Balancing Profitability with Social Responsibility

As the discussion delved deeper, Emma turned the board's attention to the delicate balance between profitability and social responsibility. She knew that in the fast-paced world of business, it was essential to strike a harmonious equilibrium between driving financial success and making a positive impact on society.

"Ladies and gentlemen, as leaders of GlobalTech Enterprises, we must recognize that our actions have far-reaching consequences beyond the bottom line," Emma began, her voice tinged with gravity. "While profitability is crucial for our company's sustainability, we must also consider our broader social responsibilities and the impact of our decisions on people, communities, and the environment."

She guided her directors through an exploration of the ethical dilemmas inherent in balancing profitability with social responsibility, highlighting the importance of ethical leadership, transparency, and stakeholder engagement in navigating these complex issues.

"We cannot afford to prioritize short-term profits at the expense of long-term sustainability," Emma explained, her eyes scanning the room. "We must take a holistic approach to decision-making, considering not only the financial implications but also the social and environmental consequences of our actions."

As she spoke, Emma could see the directors nodding in agreement, their expressions reflecting a growing awareness of the interconnectedness of business and society. They understood that as leaders, they had a duty to consider the broader impact of their decisions and strive to create value not just for shareholders, but for all stakeholders.

"But achieving the delicate balance between profitability and social responsibility requires more than just good intentions—it requires action," Emma continued, her voice growing more serious. "We need to embed social responsibility into our business strategy, operations, and culture, and hold ourselves accountable for making a positive impact on the world."

She then outlined strategies for effectively balancing profitability with social responsibility, from adopting sustainable business practices and supporting community initiatives to engaging with stakeholders and measuring and reporting on social and environmental performance.

"As leaders, it's our responsibility to demonstrate that profitability and social responsibility are not mutually exclusive, but complementary," Emma declared, her tone unwavering. "By prioritizing social responsibility in our decision-making processes, we can build trust, enhance our reputation, and create long-term value for our company and society."

As the discussion unfolded, Emma could sense a palpable determination in the room. The directors, once focused solely on financial performance, were now embracing the broader implications of their actions, recognizing that profitability and social responsibility were not conflicting goals, but interconnected pillars of sustainable business success.

"With a commitment to balancing profitability with social responsibility, we can lead by example and inspire positive change in our industry and beyond," Emma concluded, her voice filled with conviction. "Let's embrace this opportunity to create a more sustainable, equitable, and prosperous future for all."

Transparency and Accountability in Data Usage

As the discussion delved deeper into the complexities of corporate responsibility, Emma steered the board's attention towards the critical importance of transparency and accountability in data usage. She understood that in the digital age, where data was increasingly becoming a currency of its own, ensuring transparency and accountability in its usage was paramount.

"Ladies and gentlemen, as stewards of GlobalTech Enterprises, we have a responsibility to handle data with the utmost care and integrity," Emma began, her voice resonating with conviction. "Transparency and accountability in data usage are not just ethical imperatives but fundamental elements of building trust with our customers and stakeholders."

She guided her directors through an exploration of the ethical implications of data usage, highlighting the risks of privacy infringement, data breaches, and misuse of personal information.

"As a technology company, we have access to vast amounts of data that can be incredibly valuable—but also incredibly sensitive," Emma explained, her eyes scanning the room. "We must ensure that our customers' data is used responsibly, ethically, and in accordance with their expectations and rights."

As she spoke, Emma could see the directors nodding in agreement, their expressions reflecting a growing recognition of the importance of data transparency and accountability. They understood that in an era of increasing data privacy concerns, failure to uphold these principles could have severe consequences for the company's reputation and bottom line.

"But ensuring transparency and accountability in data usage is not just about compliance—it's also about building trust," Emma continued, her voice growing more serious. "We need to be transparent about how we collect, use, and protect data, and be held accountable for our actions."

She then outlined strategies for effectively ensuring transparency and accountability in data usage, from implementing clear data usage policies and procedures to providing transparent disclosures about data practices and seeking consent for data collection and processing.

"As leaders, it's our responsibility to foster a culture of transparency and accountability in data usage within our organization," Emma declared, her tone unwavering. "By prioritizing these principles, we can build trust with our customers, strengthen our relationships with stakeholders, and differentiate ourselves as a company that respects privacy and values integrity."

As the discussion unfolded, Emma could sense a palpable determination in the room. The directors, once focused solely on technological innovation, were now embracing the ethical imperative of responsible data usage, recognizing it as essential to their role as custodians of GlobalTech Enterprises' reputation and success.

"With a commitment to transparency and accountability in

data usage, we can build trust, enhance our reputation, and create long-term value for our company and stakeholders," Emma concluded, her voice filled with confidence. "Let's embrace this opportunity to lead by example and demonstrate our commitment to ethical data practices in the digital age."

Ethical Decision-Making Frameworks for Digital Governance

As the discussion progressed, Emma directed the board's attention to the critical task of implementing ethical decision-making frameworks for digital governance. She understood that in the rapidly evolving landscape of technology, where ethical dilemmas were increasingly complex, having clear frameworks in place was essential for guiding responsible decision-making.

"Ladies and gentlemen, as we navigate the complexities of digital governance, it's imperative that we have robust ethical decision-making frameworks in place to guide our actions," Emma began, her voice carrying a sense of urgency. "These frameworks will serve as our compass, helping us navigate the ethical challenges inherent in our technological advancements."

She guided her directors through an exploration of the importance of ethical decision-making frameworks, highlighting their role in promoting consistency, accountability, and transparency in decision-making processes.

"As leaders of GlobalTech Enterprises, we must ensure that our decisions are not only legally compliant but also ethically sound," Emma explained, her eyes scanning the room. "Ethical decision-making frameworks provide us with a structured approach to evaluating the ethical implications of our actions and making decisions that align with our values and principles."

As she spoke, Emma could see the directors nodding in agreement, their expressions reflecting a growing understanding of the significance of ethical frameworks in guiding responsible behavior. They understood that in the digital age, where ethical dilemmas were increasingly prevalent, having clear guidelines was essential for fostering a culture of integrity and accountability.

"But implementing ethical decision-making frameworks is not just about creating policies—it's also about fostering a culture of ethical leadership," Emma continued, her voice growing more serious. "We need to empower our employees to recognize ethical dilemmas, speak up when they see wrongdoing, and make decisions that prioritize ethical considerations."

She then outlined strategies for effectively implementing ethical decision-making frameworks, from providing training and resources on ethical decision-making to establishing mechanisms for ethical review and oversight.

"As leaders, it's our responsibility to ensure that our company operates with the highest standards of ethics and integrity," Emma declared, her tone unwavering. "By prioritizing ethical decision-making frameworks, we can build trust with our customers, enhance our reputation, and create a culture where ethical considerations are at the forefront of everything we do."

As the discussion unfolded, Emma could sense a palpable determination in the room. The directors, once focused solely on financial performance, were now embracing the broader implications of their actions, recognizing that ethical decision-making was not just a moral imperative, but a strategic imperative for long-term success.

"With a commitment to ethical decision-making frameworks, we can lead by example and inspire positive change in our industry and beyond," Emma concluded, her voice filled with conviction. "Let's embrace this opportunity to create a culture where ethics are not just a part of what we do, but who we are."

Engaging Stakeholders in Ethical Dialogues

As the discussion deepened, Emma emphasized the critical importance of engaging stakeholders in ethical dialogues. She recognized that in the digital age, where technology increasingly intersects with society, the perspectives and concerns of stakeholders must be considered in ethical decision-making processes.

"Ladies and gentlemen, as leaders of GlobalTech Enterprises, we must recognize that our decisions impact a wide range of stakeholders, from customers and employees to communities and regulators," Emma began, her voice resonating with conviction. "Engaging stakeholders in ethical dialogues is essential for understanding their perspectives, addressing their concerns, and ensuring that our decisions reflect their values and interests."

She guided her directors through an exploration of the importance of stakeholder engagement in ethical decision-making, highlighting its role in building trust, fostering collaboration, and enhancing legitimacy.

"As a technology company, we have a responsibility to consider the broader societal implications of our actions,"

Emma explained, her eyes scanning the room. "Engaging stakeholders in ethical dialogues allows us to tap into their expertise, gain valuable insights, and co-create solutions that benefit not only our company but also society as a whole."

As she spoke, Emma could see the directors nodding in agreement, their expressions reflecting a growing recognition of the importance of stakeholder engagement in ethical decision-making. They understood that by actively involving stakeholders in the decision-making process, they could build stronger relationships, mitigate risks, and enhance their company's reputation.

"But engaging stakeholders in ethical dialogues is not just about consultation—it's also about collaboration," Emma continued, her voice growing more serious. "We need to create spaces for meaningful dialogue, where diverse perspectives are heard, respected, and integrated into our decision-making processes."

She then outlined strategies for effectively engaging stakeholders in ethical dialogues, from conducting stakeholder consultations and listening sessions to establishing advisory boards and multi-stakeholder partnerships.

"As leaders, it's our responsibility to create opportunities for stakeholders to actively participate in ethical decision-making," Emma declared, her tone unwavering. "By prioritizing stakeholder engagement, we can build trust, foster collaboration, and create solutions that reflect the diverse perspectives and values of our stakeholders."

As the discussion unfolded, Emma could sense a palpable determination in the room. The directors, once focused solely on internal processes, were now embracing the broader implications of their actions, recognizing that by engaging stakeholders in ethical dialogues, they could create more inclusive, sustainable, and responsible outcomes.

"With a commitment to engaging stakeholders in ethical dialogues, we can lead by example and inspire positive change in our industry and beyond," Emma concluded, her voice filled with conviction. "Let's embrace this opportunity to build trust, foster collaboration, and create a better future for all."

5

Chapter Five: Innovative Governance Structures and Practices

"Forging Tomorrow: Pioneering Innovative Governance Structures and Practices"

In the boardroom of GlobalTech Enterprises, Emma Carter stood at the forefront of a pivotal discussion on innovative governance structures and practices. With the rapid evolution of technology and business landscapes, Emma understood that traditional governance models were no longer sufficient to meet the demands of the digital age.

"Ladies and gentlemen, welcome to a new era of governance," Emma began, her voice imbued with a sense of excitement and determination. "As we stand on the cusp of unprecedented technological advancements, it's time for us to reimagine governance and embrace innovative structures and practices that will propel GlobalTech Enterprises into the future."

She guided her directors through an exploration of the need for innovative governance structures and practices,

CHAPTER FIVE: INNOVATIVE GOVERNANCE STRUCTURES AND PRACTICES

highlighting the challenges posed by the digital age and the opportunities for transformation and growth.

"Innovation is the lifeblood of our company, and it must also permeate our governance processes," Emma explained, her eyes shining with enthusiasm. "We need governance structures that are agile, adaptive, and responsive to change, allowing us to capitalize on emerging opportunities and navigate evolving risks with confidence."

As she spoke, Emma could see the directors leaning forward in their seats, their expressions reflecting a growing excitement and anticipation. They understood that by embracing innovative governance structures and practices, they could position GlobalTech Enterprises as a leader in the digital age, driving innovation, agility, and sustainable growth.

"But innovation in governance is not just about adopting new technologies—it's also about fostering a culture of innovation and experimentation," Emma continued, her voice growing more serious. "We need to create an environment where new ideas are encouraged, failures are embraced as learning opportunities, and unconventional thinking is celebrated."

She then outlined strategies for fostering innovative governance structures and practices, from establishing cross-functional teams and agile decision-making processes to implementing digital tools and analytics for real-time monitoring and risk management.

"As leaders, it's our responsibility to champion innovation in governance and create a culture where creativity and experimentation thrive," Emma declared, her tone unwavering. "By prioritizing innovative governance structures and practices, we can unlock new opportunities, drive sustainable growth, and create value for our company and stakeholders."

As the discussion unfolded, Emma could sense a palpable energy in the room. The directors, once accustomed to traditional governance models, were now embracing the idea of innovation as a catalyst for change and growth, recognizing it as essential to their role as stewards of GlobalTech Enterprises' future.

"With a commitment to innovative governance structures and practices, we can forge a path to a brighter tomorrow for GlobalTech Enterprises," Emma concluded, her voice filled with optimism. "Let's embrace this opportunity to lead with courage, creativity, and vision, and chart a course towards success in the digital age."

Exploring Agile and Decentralized Governance Models

As the discussion delved deeper into innovative governance structures, Emma turned the board's attention to the exploration of agile and decentralized governance models. She knew that in the fast-paced, dynamic landscape of the digital age, traditional hierarchical structures were often too rigid to respond effectively to emerging challenges and opportunities.

"Ladies and gentlemen, as we embark on our journey of innovation in governance, it's essential that we explore agile and decentralized models that can adapt to the rapid pace of change," Emma began, her voice filled with conviction. "These models offer the flexibility and responsiveness we need to thrive in the ever-evolving digital landscape."

She guided her directors through an exploration of the principles of agile and decentralized governance, highlighting their ability to empower teams, foster collaboration, and drive decision-making closer to the point of impact.

CHAPTER FIVE: INNOVATIVE GOVERNANCE STRUCTURES AND PRACTICES

"Agile governance is not just about speed—it's about flexibility, adaptability, and resilience," Emma explained, her eyes shining with enthusiasm. "By breaking down silos, empowering cross-functional teams, and embracing iterative approaches, we can make faster, more informed decisions and respond more effectively to changing market dynamics."

As she spoke, Emma could see the directors nodding in agreement, their expressions reflecting a growing recognition of the potential of agile governance to drive innovation and competitiveness. They understood that by embracing agile principles, they could unleash the full potential of GlobalTech Enterprises' talent and resources.

"But agile governance is just one piece of the puzzle—decentralized governance offers another perspective on how we can distribute decision-making authority and accountability across the organization," Emma continued, her voice growing more serious. "By empowering teams and individuals to make decisions autonomously within clear guidelines and objectives, we can foster a culture of ownership, accountability, and innovation at every level of the organization."

She then outlined strategies for exploring agile and decentralized governance models, from piloting agile teams and cross-functional task forces to implementing decentralized decision-making frameworks and accountability mechanisms.

"As leaders, it's our responsibility to challenge the status quo and explore new ways of working that align with the realities of the digital age," Emma declared, her tone unwavering. "By prioritizing agile and decentralized governance models, we can unlock the full potential of our organization, drive innovation, and create value for our company and stakeholders."

As the discussion unfolded, Emma could sense a palpable

excitement in the room. The directors, once accustomed to traditional top-down decision-making, were now embracing the idea of distributed authority and collaborative decision-making, recognizing it as essential to their role as leaders in the digital age.

"With a commitment to exploring agile and decentralized governance models, we can pave the way for a more dynamic, responsive, and innovative GlobalTech Enterprises," Emma concluded, her voice filled with optimism. "Let's embrace this opportunity to reimagine governance and shape a future where agility and decentralization are the hallmarks of our success."

Incorporating AI and Machine Learning in Governance Processes

As the discussion progressed, Emma directed the board's attention to the integration of AI and machine learning in governance processes. She understood that in the era of rapid technological advancement, harnessing the power of AI and machine learning could revolutionize governance, enabling more informed decision-making and proactive risk management.

"Ladies and gentlemen, as we explore innovative governance structures, it's imperative that we leverage the transformative potential of AI and machine learning," Emma began, her voice filled with anticipation. "These technologies offer unprecedented opportunities to enhance efficiency, effectiveness, and transparency in our governance processes."

She guided her directors through an exploration of the capabilities of AI and machine learning, highlighting their ability to analyze vast amounts of data, identify patterns and trends, and generate insights to support decision-making.

"AI and machine learning have the potential to revolutionize how we govern our organization," Emma explained, her eyes shining with excitement. "By automating routine tasks, augmenting human intelligence, and predicting future outcomes, these technologies can enable us to make better, more informed decisions and anticipate risks before they escalate."

As she spoke, Emma could see the directors nodding in agreement, their expressions reflecting a growing recognition of the transformative potential of AI and machine learning. They understood that by embracing these technologies, they could unlock new levels of efficiency and effectiveness in governance processes.

"But incorporating AI and machine learning in governance processes is not just about adopting new tools—it's also about building trust and ensuring accountability," Emma continued, her voice growing more serious. "We need to be transparent about how these technologies are used, ensure they are ethically and responsibly deployed, and hold ourselves accountable for the outcomes."

She then outlined strategies for effectively incorporating AI and machine learning in governance processes, from investing in AI-driven analytics and predictive modeling to establishing governance frameworks for AI ethics and accountability.

"As leaders, it's our responsibility to harness the power of AI and machine learning for the benefit of our organization and stakeholders," Emma declared, her tone unwavering. "By prioritizing the responsible integration of these technologies, we can drive innovation, enhance decision-making, and create value for our company and stakeholders."

As the discussion unfolded, Emma could sense a palpable excitement in the room. The directors, once hesitant about the complexities of AI and machine learning, were now embracing the idea of leveraging these technologies to transform governance, recognizing it as essential to their role as leaders in the digital age.

"With a commitment to incorporating AI and machine learning in governance processes, we can unlock new opportunities and pave the way for a more agile, informed, and resilient GlobalTech Enterprises," Emma concluded, her voice filled with optimism. "Let's embrace this opportunity to harness the power of technology and shape a future where innovation drives our success."

Leveraging Blockchain for Transparent Governance

As the discussion delved deeper into innovative governance practices, Emma turned the board's attention to the potential of leveraging blockchain technology for transparent governance. She knew that blockchain, with its decentralized and immutable ledger system, had the power to revolutionize transparency and accountability in governance processes.

"Ladies and gentlemen, as we continue our exploration of innovative governance structures, let us consider the transformative potential of blockchain technology," Emma began, her voice resonating with anticipation. "Blockchain offers us the opportunity to create a new paradigm of transparency and accountability in governance, one that is decentralized, tamper-proof, and accessible to all stakeholders."

She guided her directors through an exploration of the

principles of blockchain technology, highlighting its ability to create a transparent and auditable record of transactions, contracts, and decisions.

"Blockchain has the potential to revolutionize how we govern our organization," Emma explained, her eyes shining with excitement. "By providing a secure and transparent ledger of governance processes, blockchain can enhance trust, reduce the risk of fraud and corruption, and empower stakeholders to verify the integrity of our decisions."

As she spoke, Emma could see the directors leaning forward in their seats, their expressions reflecting a growing recognition of the transformative potential of blockchain. They understood that by embracing this technology, they could usher in a new era of transparency and accountability in governance.

"But leveraging blockchain for transparent governance is not just about adopting new technology—it's also about reimagining our governance processes and building consensus among stakeholders," Emma continued, her voice growing more serious. "We need to collaborate with regulators, industry partners, and other stakeholders to develop standards and best practices for blockchain governance and ensure that our use of this technology aligns with our values and principles."

She then outlined strategies for effectively leveraging blockchain for transparent governance, from implementing blockchain-based voting systems and smart contracts to establishing governance frameworks for blockchain governance.

"As leaders, it's our responsibility to harness the power of blockchain for the benefit of our organization and stakeholders," Emma declared, her tone unwavering. "By prioritizing transparent governance practices, we can build trust, enhance accountability, and create value for our company and stakeholders."

As the discussion unfolded, Emma could sense a palpable excitement in the room. The directors, once skeptical about the complexities of blockchain, were now embracing the idea of leveraging this technology to transform governance, recognizing it as essential to their role as leaders in the digital age.

"With a commitment to leveraging blockchain for transparent governance, we can usher in a new era of trust and accountability at GlobalTech Enterprises," Emma concluded, her voice filled with optimism. "Let's embrace this opportunity to harness the power of technology and shape a future where transparency is the cornerstone of our success."

Smart Contracts and Automated Compliance Mechanisms

As the discussion progressed, Emma shifted the board's focus to the potential of smart contracts and automated compliance mechanisms in governance practices. She knew that in the era of rapid technological advancement, these innovations could streamline processes, reduce human error, and ensure compliance with regulations.

"Ladies and gentlemen, as we delve deeper into innovative governance practices, let us explore the transformative power of smart contracts and automated compliance mechanisms," Emma began, her voice infused with anticipation. "These technologies offer us the opportunity to revolutionize our governance processes, making them more efficient, transparent, and compliant."

She guided her directors through an exploration of smart contracts, highlighting their ability to automatically execute and enforce agreements based on predefined rules and conditions.

"Smart contracts have the potential to streamline our governance processes, reducing the need for intermediaries and eliminating the risk of human error," Emma explained, her eyes shining with excitement. "By encoding governance rules and procedures into self-executing contracts, we can ensure compliance with regulations, reduce costs, and accelerate decision-making."

As she spoke, Emma could see the directors nodding in agreement, their expressions reflecting a growing recognition of the transformative potential of smart contracts. They understood that by embracing this technology, they could simplify complex governance processes and increase efficiency.

"But smart contracts are just the beginning—automated compliance mechanisms offer another layer of innovation in governance practices," Emma continued, her voice growing more serious. "By leveraging AI and machine learning, we can automate the monitoring and enforcement of regulatory requirements, reducing the risk of non-compliance and enhancing trust with regulators and stakeholders."

She then outlined strategies for effectively implementing smart contracts and automated compliance mechanisms, from identifying key governance processes suitable for automation to partnering with technology providers and experts in regulatory compliance.

"As leaders, it's our responsibility to embrace innovation and leverage technology to enhance our governance practices,"

Emma declared, her tone unwavering. "By prioritizing smart contracts and automated compliance mechanisms, we can streamline our operations, reduce risks, and create value for our company and stakeholders."

As the discussion unfolded, Emma could sense a palpable excitement in the room. The directors, once hesitant about the complexities of technology, were now embracing the idea of leveraging smart contracts and automated compliance mechanisms to transform governance, recognizing it as essential to their role as leaders in the digital age.

"With a commitment to smart contracts and automated compliance mechanisms, we can usher in a new era of efficiency and compliance at GlobalTech Enterprises," Emma concluded, her voice filled with optimism. "Let's embrace this opportunity to harness the power of technology and shape a future where governance is not just smarter, but also more effective and resilient."

Crowdsoursing Governance Ideas and Feedback

As the discussion in the boardroom unfolded, Emma turned the board's attention to the innovative concept of crowdsourcing governance ideas and feedback. She knew that in the era of rapid technological advancement and interconnectedness, tapping into the collective intelligence of stakeholders could yield invaluable insights and foster greater engagement in governance processes.

"Ladies and gentlemen, as we explore innovative governance practices, let us consider the power of crowdsourcing ideas and feedback from our stakeholders," Emma began, her voice brimming with enthusiasm. "Crowdsourcing offers us the opportunity to harness the collective wisdom and creativity of our employees, customers, and partners, enabling us to co-create governance solutions that are truly responsive to their needs and aspirations."

She guided her directors through an exploration of the principles of crowdsourcing, highlighting its ability to democratize decision-making, foster collaboration, and generate fresh perspectives and ideas.

"Crowdsourcing governance ideas and feedback can help us tap into the diverse expertise and experiences of our stakeholders, empowering them to actively participate in shaping the future of our organization," Emma explained, her eyes shining with excitement. "By creating platforms and mechanisms for open dialogue and collaboration, we can build trust, foster engagement, and enhance the legitimacy of our governance processes."

As she spoke, Emma could see the directors nodding in agreement, their expressions reflecting a growing recognition of the transformative potential of crowdsourcing. They understood that by embracing this approach, they could tap into untapped sources of creativity and innovation, driving more inclusive and effective governance practices.

"But crowdsourcing governance ideas and feedback is not just about soliciting input—it's also about listening, responding, and acting on the insights we receive," Emma continued, her voice growing more serious. "We need to create a culture where feedback is valued, and stakeholders feel empowered to contribute their ideas and perspectives without fear of reprisal."

She then outlined strategies for effectively implementing crowdsourcing initiatives, from launching online platforms and surveys to hosting town hall meetings and focus groups.

"As leaders, it's our responsibility to create opportunities for meaningful engagement and collaboration with our stakeholders," Emma declared, her tone unwavering. "By prioritizing crowdsourcing governance ideas and feedback, we can harness the collective intelligence of our stakeholders, drive innovation, and create value for our company and stakeholders."

As the discussion unfolded, Emma could sense a palpable excitement in the room. The directors, once focused solely on internal processes, were now embracing the idea of engaging stakeholders in governance, recognizing it as essential to their role as leaders in the digital age.

"With a commitment to crowdsourcing governance ideas and feedback, we can foster a culture of openness, collaboration, and innovation at GlobalTech Enterprises," Emma concluded, her voice filled with optimism. "Let's embrace this opportunity to harness the power of collective intelligence and shape a future where governance is truly participatory and inclusive."

Case Studies: Companies at the Forefront of Innovative Governance

As the discussion in the boardroom continued, Emma turned the attention of the directors to case studies of companies at the forefront of innovative governance practices. She knew that real-world examples could provide valuable insights and inspiration for GlobalTech Enterprises as they embarked on their journey of transformation.

"Ladies and gentlemen, as we explore innovative governance

practices, let us draw inspiration from companies that are leading the way in this area," Emma began, her voice filled with anticipation. "By studying their experiences and learning from their successes and challenges, we can gain valuable insights that will inform our own governance journey."

She guided her directors through a series of case studies, each highlighting a company that had successfully implemented innovative governance practices.

"The first case study is Airbnb," Emma explained, her eyes shining with excitement. "As a platform-based business operating in the sharing economy, Airbnb has pioneered new approaches to governance that prioritize transparency, accountability, and community engagement."

She then detailed Airbnb's approach to governance, from its transparent host and guest reviews to its community-driven policies and decision-making processes.

"The second case study is Microsoft," Emma continued, her voice brimming with enthusiasm. "Under the leadership of Satya Nadella, Microsoft has undergone a remarkable transformation, embracing agile principles, decentralized decision-making, and a growth mindset."

She then outlined Microsoft's journey towards innovative governance, from its adoption of agile practices to its commitment to diversity and inclusion in decision-making.

"The third case study is Patagonia," Emma explained, her tone becoming more serious. "As a company committed to environmental and social responsibility, Patagonia has implemented governance practices that prioritize sustainability, ethical sourcing, and stakeholder engagement."

She then detailed Patagonia's approach to governance, from its transparent supply chain practices to its activism on environmental issues.

"As leaders, it's essential that we draw inspiration from companies like Airbnb, Microsoft, and Patagonia," Emma declared, her tone unwavering. "By studying their experiences and learning from their successes and challenges, we can chart a course towards innovative governance practices that will drive our success in the digital age."

As the discussion unfolded, Emma could sense a palpable energy in the room. The directors, once focused solely on internal processes, were now inspired by the real-world examples of companies that had successfully embraced innovative governance practices.

"With a commitment to learning from the experiences of others, we can position GlobalTech Enterprises as a leader in innovative governance," Emma concluded, her voice filled with optimism. "Let's embrace this opportunity to learn, grow, and innovate together, and shape a future where governance is a driver of success and sustainability."

6

Chapter Six: Digital Transformation Strategy and Oversight

"Navigating the Digital Frontier: Crafting a Digital Transformation Strategy with Oversight"

In the boardroom of GlobalTech Enterprises, Emma Carter stood poised to lead the discussion on digital transformation strategy and oversight. With the rapid pace of technological advancement shaping the business landscape, she knew that crafting a comprehensive strategy with effective oversight was essential for the company's success in the digital age.

"Ladies and gentlemen, welcome to a pivotal discussion on our digital transformation strategy and oversight," Emma began, her voice resonating with authority. "As we navigate the ever-changing digital frontier, it's imperative that we chart a course that aligns with our vision, values, and long-term objectives."

She guided her directors through an exploration of the key

components of a digital transformation strategy, highlighting the importance of clarity, alignment, and agility in driving success.

"Our digital transformation strategy must be anchored in a clear understanding of our business objectives, market dynamics, and competitive landscape," Emma explained, her eyes scanning the room. "It should prioritize investments in technology, talent, and processes that will enable us to innovate, differentiate, and create value for our customers and stakeholders."

As she spoke, Emma could see the directors nodding in agreement, their expressions reflecting a growing understanding of the strategic imperative of digital transformation. They understood that in the digital age, where disruption is the norm, embracing transformation was essential for survival and growth.

"But crafting a digital transformation strategy is just the beginning—effective oversight is essential for ensuring its successful execution and alignment with our strategic objectives," Emma continued, her voice growing more serious. "We need to establish clear governance structures, processes, and metrics for monitoring progress, mitigating risks, and ensuring accountability at every stage of the journey."

She then outlined strategies for effective oversight of the digital transformation strategy, from establishing a dedicated oversight committee to implementing regular performance reviews and risk assessments.

"As leaders, it's our responsibility to provide the guidance and support necessary to drive the successful execution of our digital transformation strategy," Emma declared, her tone unwavering. "By prioritizing effective oversight, we can ensure that our investments in technology and innovation deliver the intended outcomes and create sustainable value for our company and stakeholders."

As the discussion unfolded, Emma could sense a palpable determination in the room. The directors, once focused solely on traditional business practices, were now embracing the imperative of digital transformation, recognizing it as essential to their role as stewards of GlobalTech Enterprises' future.

"With a commitment to crafting a comprehensive digital transformation strategy with effective oversight, we can navigate the digital frontier with confidence and achieve our vision for success in the digital age," Emma concluded, her voice filled with optimism. "Let's embrace this opportunity to lead with courage, vision, and determination, and shape a future where innovation drives our success."

Aligning Digital Strategy with Corporate Goals

As the discussion in the boardroom continued, Emma shifted the focus to the critical task of aligning the digital strategy with corporate goals. She knew that without this alignment, even the most well-crafted digital transformation strategy could falter, leading to missed opportunities and wasted resources.

"Ladies and gentlemen, as we delve deeper into our digital transformation strategy, it's essential that we ensure alignment with our corporate goals," Emma began, her voice firm with conviction. "Our digital initiatives must be directly linked to our overarching objectives, ensuring that every investment and decision contributes to our long-term success."

She guided her directors through an exploration of the importance of alignment, highlighting the need for clarity, consistency, and commitment in translating corporate goals into actionable digital initiatives.

"Our digital strategy should not exist in a vacuum—it must be tightly integrated with our corporate strategy, reflecting our mission, values, and priorities," Emma explained, her eyes scanning the room. "We need to identify the key business drivers that will shape our digital journey and ensure that every initiative we undertake aligns with these drivers."

As she spoke, Emma could see the directors nodding in agreement, their expressions reflecting a growing understanding of the strategic imperative of alignment. They understood that without a clear connection between digital efforts and corporate goals, the company risked losing sight of its purpose and direction.

"But aligning our digital strategy with corporate goals is not just about mapping initiatives to objectives—it's also about fostering a culture of alignment throughout the organization," Emma continued, her voice growing more serious. "We need to communicate our strategic priorities clearly and consistently, ensuring that every employee understands how their work contributes to our collective success."

She then outlined strategies for ensuring alignment between the digital strategy and corporate goals, from conducting regular strategic reviews and performance evaluations to fostering cross-functional collaboration and communication.

"As leaders, it's our responsibility to champion alignment and ensure that our digital initiatives are driving us closer to our corporate goals," Emma declared, her tone unwavering. "By prioritizing alignment, we can maximize the impact of our digital investments, mitigate risks, and create sustainable value for our company and stakeholders."

As the discussion unfolded, Emma could sense a palpable determination in the room. The directors, once focused solely on digital technology, were now embracing the importance of aligning their efforts with corporate goals, recognizing it as essential to their role as leaders in the digital age.

"With a commitment to aligning our digital strategy with corporate goals, we can chart a course towards success in the digital age," Emma concluded, her voice filled with optimism. "Let's embrace this opportunity to lead with clarity, purpose, and alignment, and shape a future where every digital initiative moves us closer to our corporate vision."

Board Oversight of Digital Transformation Initiatives

As the discussion unfolded in the boardroom, Emma directed the attention of the directors to the crucial aspect of board oversight of digital transformation initiatives. She understood that effective oversight was essential for ensuring that digital investments delivered value, mitigating risks, and maintaining alignment with corporate goals.

"Ladies and gentlemen, as we continue to refine our digital transformation strategy, it's imperative that we establish robust board oversight of our digital initiatives," Emma began, her voice resonating with authority. "The board plays a critical role in providing guidance, accountability, and strategic direction to ensure the success of our digital transformation journey."

She guided her directors through an exploration of the responsibilities of board oversight, highlighting the need for regular monitoring, evaluation, and adjustment of digital initiatives to ensure alignment with corporate goals and objectives.

"Our board oversight of digital transformation initiatives must be proactive, strategic, and informed," Emma explained, her eyes scanning the room. "We need to establish clear governance structures, processes, and metrics for assessing the progress, performance, and impact of our digital initiatives."

As she spoke, Emma could see the directors nodding in agreement, their expressions reflecting a growing understanding of the importance of board oversight. They understood that without effective oversight, the company risked losing control of its digital investments and veering off course from its strategic objectives.

"But board oversight of digital transformation initiatives is not just about monitoring progress—it's also about providing guidance and support to ensure that our digital initiatives are delivering value and driving us closer to our corporate goals," Emma continued, her voice growing more serious. "We need to actively engage with management, asking the tough questions, challenging assumptions, and ensuring that risks are identified and addressed in a timely manner."

She then outlined strategies for effective board oversight of digital transformation initiatives, from establishing a dedicated oversight committee to conducting regular reviews and risk assessments.

"As leaders, it's our responsibility to ensure that our digital transformation initiatives are aligned with our strategic objectives and delivering value to our company and stakeholders," Emma declared, her tone unwavering. "By prioritizing effective board oversight, we can mitigate risks, maximize opportunities, and create sustainable value for our company in the digital age."

As the discussion unfolded, Emma could sense a palpable determination in the room. The directors, once focused solely on traditional business practices, were now embracing their role in providing strategic guidance and oversight of digital transformation initiatives, recognizing it as essential to their stewardship of GlobalTech Enterprises' future.

"With a commitment to robust board oversight of digital transformation initiatives, we can navigate the complexities of the digital landscape with confidence and achieve our vision for success," Emma concluded, her voice filled with optimism. "Let's embrace this opportunity to lead with clarity, accountability, and foresight, and shape a future where digital transformation is a driver of sustainable growth and innovation."

Risk Assessment and Management in Digital Projects

As the discussion continued in the boardroom, Emma shifted the focus to the critical aspect of risk assessment and management in digital projects. She knew that in the fast-paced world of digital transformation, identifying and mitigating risks was essential for safeguarding the company's interests and ensuring the success of its initiatives.

"Ladies and gentlemen, as we navigate the complexities of digital transformation, it's imperative that we prioritize risk assessment and management in our digital projects," Emma began, her voice firm with conviction. "The rapid pace of technological change brings with it a multitude of risks, from cybersecurity threats to operational disruptions, that can impact the success of our initiatives."

She guided her directors through an exploration of the

importance of risk assessment, highlighting the need for a systematic approach to identify, analyze, and mitigate risks throughout the lifecycle of digital projects.

"Our risk assessment and management processes must be comprehensive, proactive, and dynamic," Emma explained, her eyes scanning the room. "We need to identify potential risks early in the planning stages of digital projects, assess their likelihood and impact, and develop strategies to mitigate or transfer them."

As she spoke, Emma could see the directors nodding in agreement, their expressions reflecting a growing understanding of the importance of risk management. They understood that without effective risk assessment and management, the company risked facing costly disruptions and setbacks in its digital initiatives.

"But risk assessment and management in digital projects is not just about avoiding negative outcomes—it's also about seizing opportunities and maximizing returns," Emma continued, her voice growing more serious. "We need to strike the right balance between risk and reward, recognizing that innovation often involves taking calculated risks to achieve our strategic objectives."

She then outlined strategies for effective risk assessment and management in digital projects, from establishing a risk management framework to conducting regular risk assessments and scenario planning exercises.

"As leaders, it's our responsibility to ensure that our digital projects are executed with a clear understanding of the risks involved and the strategies in place to manage them," Emma declared, her tone unwavering. "By prioritizing risk assessment and management, we can safeguard the success of our digital initiatives and create sustainable value for our company and stakeholders."

As the discussion unfolded, Emma could sense a palpable determination in the room. The directors, once focused solely on the opportunities of digital transformation, were now embracing the importance of managing its inherent risks, recognizing it as essential to their stewardship of GlobalTech Enterprises' future.

"With a commitment to robust risk assessment and management in our digital projects, we can navigate the uncertainties of the digital landscape with confidence and achieve our vision for success," Emma concluded, her voice filled with optimism. "Let's embrace this opportunity to lead with foresight, resilience, and agility, and shape a future where digital transformation is a source of sustainable growth and competitive advantage."

Monitoring Key Performance Indicators (KPIs) for Digital Success

As the discussion continued to unfold in the boardroom, Emma shifted the focus to the critical aspect of monitoring key performance indicators (KPIs) for digital success. She understood that in the rapidly evolving landscape of digital transformation, tracking KPIs was essential for assessing progress, identifying areas for improvement, and ensuring that digital initiatives were delivering value to the organization.

"Ladies and gentlemen, as we embark on our digital transformation journey, it's imperative that we establish robust mechanisms for monitoring key performance indicators to gauge our progress and ensure success," Emma began, her voice projecting authority. "The digital age presents us with unprecedented opportunities, but also challenges, and it's essential that we have a clear understanding of how our digital initiatives are contributing to our strategic objectives."

She guided her directors through an exploration of the importance of monitoring KPIs, emphasizing the need for alignment with corporate goals, relevance, and timeliness in selecting and tracking metrics.

"Our KPIs must be directly tied to our strategic objectives and provide us with actionable insights into the effectiveness of our digital initiatives," Emma explained, her eyes scanning the room. "We need to establish clear targets, benchmarks, and thresholds for each KPI, allowing us to measure progress, identify trends, and make data-driven decisions."

As she spoke, Emma could see the directors nodding in agreement, their expressions reflecting a growing understanding of the importance of KPI monitoring. They understood that without a clear understanding of how their digital initiatives were performing, the company risked losing sight of its strategic goals and objectives.

"But monitoring KPIs is not just about collecting data—it's also about translating insights into action," Emma continued, her voice growing more serious. "We need to establish processes for regular review and analysis of KPI data, ensuring that we identify opportunities for optimization and improvement in our digital initiatives."

She then outlined strategies for effective KPI monitoring, from establishing dashboards and reporting mechanisms to conducting regular performance reviews and deep dives into KPI data.

"As leaders, it's our responsibility to ensure that our digital initiatives are delivering the intended outcomes and creating value for our company and stakeholders," Emma declared, her tone unwavering. "By prioritizing the monitoring of key performance indicators, we can track our progress, identify areas for improvement, and drive continuous innovation and growth in the digital age."

As the discussion unfolded, Emma could sense a palpable determination in the room. The directors, once focused solely on the opportunities of digital transformation, were now embracing the importance of monitoring KPIs, recognizing it as essential to their stewardship of GlobalTech Enterprises' future.

"With a commitment to robust monitoring of key performance indicators, we can navigate the complexities of the digital landscape with confidence and achieve our vision for success," Emma concluded, her voice filled with optimism. "Let's embrace this opportunity to lead with clarity, insight, and accountability, and shape a future where digital transformation is a driver of sustainable growth and competitive advantage."

Integrating Digital and Traditional Business Models

As the discussion in the boardroom progressed, Emma directed the attention of the directors to the crucial aspect of integrating digital and traditional business models. She knew that in the dynamic landscape of digital transformation, harmonizing these two paradigms was essential for leveraging the strengths of each while adapting to the changing needs of the market.

"Ladies and gentlemen, as we navigate the complexities of

digital transformation, it's imperative that we explore ways to seamlessly integrate digital and traditional business models," Emma began, her voice resonating with authority. "While digital technologies offer us unprecedented opportunities for innovation and growth, we must also recognize the enduring value of our traditional business models and seek to leverage their strengths in our digital journey."

She guided her directors through an exploration of the importance of integration, highlighting the need for synergy, agility, and customer-centricity in bridging the gap between digital and traditional business models.

"Our approach to digital transformation should not be about replacing our traditional business models with digital alternatives, but rather about integrating them in a way that creates value for our customers and stakeholders," Emma explained, her eyes scanning the room. "We need to identify areas of synergy between digital and traditional business models, leveraging the strengths of each to deliver a seamless and cohesive experience for our customers."

As she spoke, Emma could see the directors nodding in agreement, their expressions reflecting a growing understanding of the importance of integration. They understood that by harmonizing digital and traditional business models, the company could capitalize on its existing assets and capabilities while embracing the opportunities of digital innovation.

"But integrating digital and traditional business models is not without its challenges—it requires a cultural shift, organizational alignment, and a willingness to embrace change," Emma continued, her voice growing more serious. "We need to foster a culture of collaboration and innovation, breaking down silos and empowering cross-functional teams to work together towards our common goals."

She then outlined strategies for effective integration of digital and traditional business models, from cross-training and upskilling employees to redesigning business processes and reimagining customer experiences.

"As leaders, it's our responsibility to champion the integration of digital and traditional business models, ensuring that we leverage the full spectrum of our capabilities to drive success in the digital age," Emma declared, her tone unwavering. "By prioritizing integration, we can unlock new opportunities for growth, innovation, and value creation, positioning our company for long-term success."

As the discussion unfolded, Emma could sense a palpable determination in the room. The directors, once focused solely on the opportunities of digital transformation, were now embracing the importance of integrating digital and traditional business models, recognizing it as essential to their stewardship of GlobalTech Enterprises' future.

"With a commitment to integrating digital and traditional business models, we can navigate the complexities of the digital landscape with confidence and achieve our vision for success," Emma concluded, her voice filled with optimism. "Let's embrace this opportunity to lead with agility, collaboration, and innovation, and shape a future where digital and traditional business models coexist harmoniously to drive sustainable growth and competitive advantage."

Anticipating Future Technological Disruptions

As the discussion in the boardroom continued, Emma shifted the focus to the crucial aspect of anticipating future technological disruptions. She understood that in the rapidly evolving landscape of digital transformation, staying ahead of technological trends and disruptions was essential for maintaining a competitive edge and future-proofing the company.

"Ladies and gentlemen, as we chart our course through the digital landscape, it's imperative that we anticipate future technological disruptions and prepare accordingly," Emma began, her voice projecting confidence. "The pace of technological change is accelerating, and we must be proactive in identifying emerging trends and disruptions that could impact our business."

She guided her directors through an exploration of the importance of anticipation, highlighting the need for foresight, flexibility, and adaptability in navigating the uncertain terrain of technological innovation.

"Our ability to anticipate future technological disruptions will be key to our success in the digital age," Emma explained, her eyes scanning the room. "We need to continuously scan the horizon for emerging technologies, trends, and market shifts that could disrupt our industry or create new opportunities for innovation and growth."

As she spoke, Emma could see the directors nodding in agreement, their expressions reflecting a growing recognition of the importance of anticipation. They understood that by staying ahead of the curve, the company could position itself as a leader in the rapidly changing digital landscape.

"But anticipating future technological disruptions is not

just about predicting the future—it's also about preparing our organization to respond effectively to change," Emma continued, her voice growing more serious. "We need to foster a culture of innovation, experimentation, and continuous learning, empowering our employees to embrace change and adapt to new technologies and ways of working."

She then outlined strategies for effective anticipation of future technological disruptions, from establishing innovation hubs and partnerships to investing in research and development and fostering a culture of curiosity and exploration.

"As leaders, it's our responsibility to ensure that our organization is prepared to navigate the uncertainties of the digital age," Emma declared, her tone unwavering. "By prioritizing anticipation, we can seize opportunities, mitigate risks, and position our company for long-term success and sustainability."

As the discussion unfolded, Emma could sense a palpable determination in the room. The directors, once focused solely on the challenges of digital transformation, were now embracing the opportunities of anticipating future technological disruptions, recognizing it as essential to their stewardship of GlobalTech Enterprises' future.

"With a commitment to anticipating future technological disruptions, we can navigate the complexities of the digital landscape with confidence and achieve our vision for success," Emma concluded, her voice filled with optimism. "Let's embrace this opportunity to lead with foresight, agility, and innovation, and shape a future where we are always one step ahead of the curve."

7

Chapter Seven: E-Governance and Shareholder Engagement

"Bridging the Divide: E-Governance and Shareholder Engagement"

In the boardroom of GlobalTech Enterprises, Emma Carter stood before the directors, ready to delve into the next chapter of their digital journey: e-governance and shareholder engagement. With the increasing importance of digital channels in corporate governance and stakeholder communication, Emma knew that embracing e-governance was essential for enhancing transparency, accountability, and shareholder engagement.

"Ladies and gentlemen, welcome to a pivotal discussion on e-governance and shareholder engagement," Emma began, her voice carrying the weight of conviction. "In the digital age, where information flows freely and stakeholders expect greater transparency and accessibility, it's imperative that we leverage digital channels to enhance our governance practices and engage with our shareholders effectively."

She guided her directors through an exploration of the principles of e-governance, highlighting the opportunities it presented for streamlining processes, increasing accessibility, and fostering greater engagement with shareholders.

"Our transition to e-governance is not just about digitizing existing processes—it's about reimagining how we communicate, collaborate, and engage with our shareholders in the digital age," Emma explained, her eyes scanning the room. "We need to embrace digital platforms and tools that enable us to provide timely, transparent, and interactive communications, empowering our shareholders to participate in our governance processes and make informed decisions."

As she spoke, Emma could see the directors nodding in agreement, their expressions reflecting a growing understanding of the transformative potential of e-governance. They understood that by embracing digital channels, the company could enhance its governance practices and build stronger relationships with its shareholders.

"But e-governance is not without its challenges—it requires a strategic approach, robust infrastructure, and a commitment to transparency and accountability," Emma continued, her voice growing more serious. "We need to ensure that our digital platforms are secure, user-friendly, and compliant with regulatory requirements, while also fostering a culture of openness and responsiveness in our interactions with shareholders."

She then outlined strategies for implementing e-governance practices, from leveraging secure online portals for shareholder communications to utilizing digital voting platforms for shareholder meetings and resolutions.

"As leaders, it's our responsibility to embrace e-governance as a means of enhancing transparency, accountability, and shareholder engagement," Emma declared, her tone unwavering. "By prioritizing e-governance, we can strengthen our governance practices, build trust with our shareholders, and create value for our company and stakeholders."

As the discussion unfolded, Emma could sense a palpable determination in the room. The directors, once focused solely on traditional governance practices, were now embracing the opportunities of e-governance, recognizing it as essential to their role as stewards of GlobalTech Enterprises' future.

"With a commitment to e-governance and shareholder engagement, we can bridge the divide between our company and its stakeholders, and shape a future where governance is transparent, inclusive, and responsive to the needs of all," Emma concluded, her voice filled with optimism. "Let's embrace this opportunity to lead with integrity, innovation, and empathy, and forge stronger bonds with our shareholders in the digital age."

Enhancing Shareholder Communication through Digital Channels

As the discussion in the boardroom continued, Emma directed the focus towards the crucial aspect of enhancing shareholder communication through digital channels. She understood that in the digital era, effective communication was key to building trust and fostering engagement with shareholders, and leveraging digital channels offered unprecedented opportunities to achieve this goal.

"Ladies and gentlemen, as we embark on our journey of

e-governance and shareholder engagement, it's imperative that we prioritize enhancing communication with our shareholders through digital channels," Emma began, her voice resonating with conviction. "In today's interconnected world, where information is readily accessible and expectations for transparency are high, we must leverage digital platforms to ensure timely, relevant, and meaningful communication with our shareholders."

She guided her directors through an exploration of the importance of enhancing shareholder communication, emphasizing the need for clarity, accessibility, and engagement in all interactions with shareholders.

"Our transition to digital channels for shareholder communication is not just about delivering information—it's about fostering meaningful dialogue, soliciting feedback, and building relationships with our shareholders," Emma explained, her eyes scanning the room. "We need to leverage digital platforms such as email newsletters, social media, and investor portals to provide regular updates on company performance, governance practices, and strategic initiatives, while also providing avenues for shareholders to engage with us and express their views."

As she spoke, Emma could see the directors nodding in agreement, their expressions reflecting a growing recognition of the importance of effective communication. They understood that by leveraging digital channels, the company could strengthen its relationship with shareholders and build trust and loyalty over time.

"But enhancing shareholder communication through digital channels requires more than just sending out messages—it requires a strategic approach, tailored content, and a commitment to responsiveness and transparency," Emma continued, her voice growing more serious. "We need to ensure that our communications are clear, concise, and relevant to our shareholders' interests and concerns, while also being open and transparent about our performance, challenges, and plans for the future."

She then outlined strategies for enhancing shareholder communication through digital channels, from developing targeted communication plans to leveraging analytics to measure engagement and effectiveness.

"As leaders, it's our responsibility to ensure that our communication with shareholders is transparent, engaging, and responsive to their needs," Emma declared, her tone unwavering. "By prioritizing digital channels for shareholder communication, we can build stronger relationships, foster trust and confidence, and create value for our company and stakeholders."

As the discussion unfolded, Emma could sense a palpable determination in the room. The directors, once focused solely on traditional modes of communication, were now embracing the opportunities of digital channels, recognizing them as essential to their role in enhancing shareholder engagement in the digital age.

"With a commitment to enhancing shareholder communication through digital channels, we can build stronger connections with our shareholders and shape a future where transparency, engagement, and trust are the hallmarks of our governance practices," Emma concluded, her voice filled with optimism. "Let's embrace this opportunity to lead with empathy, innovation, and integrity, and foster a culture of openness and collaboration with our shareholders."

E-Voting and Shareholder Participation in Governance

In the midst of the boardroom's intensity, Emma's gaze shifted towards the next crucial aspect of their digital governance journey: e-voting and shareholder participation. She understood that empowering shareholders through digital means was essential for fostering inclusivity and strengthening corporate governance practices.

"Ladies and gentlemen, as we delve deeper into our e-governance initiatives, it's imperative that we discuss e-voting and shareholder participation in governance," Emma began, her voice resonating with purpose. "In the digital age, where connectivity knows no bounds, we must leverage technology to facilitate shareholder engagement and empower them to play a more active role in our governance processes."

She guided her directors through an exploration of the importance of e-voting and shareholder participation, emphasizing the need for accessibility, convenience, and transparency in enabling shareholders to exercise their rights and responsibilities.

"Our transition to e-voting and enhanced shareholder participation is not just about embracing new technology—it's about democratizing our governance processes and giving shareholders a voice in the decisions that affect them," Emma explained, her eyes scanning the room. "We need to leverage digital platforms and tools to enable shareholders to cast their votes electronically, participate in shareholder meetings remotely, and engage with us on key governance issues in real-time."

As she spoke, Emma could see the directors nodding in agreement, their expressions reflecting a growing understanding of the transformative potential of e-voting and shareholder participation. They understood that by embracing digital channels, the company could empower shareholders and strengthen its governance practices.

"But e-voting and shareholder participation require more than just technological infrastructure—they require a commitment to transparency, accountability, and shareholder rights," Emma continued, her voice growing more serious. "We need to ensure that our e-voting platforms are secure, user-friendly, and compliant with regulatory requirements, while also providing shareholders with clear information and opportunities to engage with us on governance matters."

She then outlined strategies for implementing e-voting and enhancing shareholder participation, from investing in secure voting platforms to conducting outreach campaigns to educate shareholders about their rights and responsibilities.

"As leaders, it's our responsibility to ensure that our governance processes are accessible, transparent, and inclusive," Emma declared, her tone unwavering. "By prioritizing e-voting and shareholder participation, we can strengthen our governance practices, build trust with our shareholders, and create value for our company and stakeholders."

As the discussion unfolded, Emma could sense a palpable determination in the room. The directors, once focused solely on traditional governance practices, were now embracing the opportunities of e-voting and shareholder participation, recognizing them as essential to their role in shaping a more inclusive and transparent future for GlobalTech Enterprises.

"With a commitment to e-voting and enhanced shareholder participation, we can empower our shareholders and strengthen our governance processes, shaping a future where governance is transparent, participatory, and accountable," Emma concluded, her voice filled with optimism. "Let's embrace this opportunity to lead with empathy, innovation, and integrity, and foster a culture of openness and collaboration with our shareholders in the digital age."

Crowdfunding and Digital Investor Engagement Platforms

As the discussion in the boardroom continued to unfold, Emma turned the attention towards another vital aspect of their digital governance strategy: crowdfunding and digital investor engagement platforms. She knew that in the era of digital transformation, democratizing investment opportunities and fostering greater investor engagement were essential for driving innovation and growth.

"Ladies and gentlemen, as we explore new avenues for shareholder participation and engagement, let's delve into the realm of crowdfunding and digital investor engagement platforms," Emma began, her voice brimming with enthusiasm. "In today's interconnected world, where capital flows freely and investors seek opportunities beyond traditional channels, we must leverage digital platforms to democratize investment and empower a broader base of stakeholders to participate in our journey."

She guided her directors through an exploration of the importance of crowdfunding and digital investor engagement, emphasizing the need for inclusivity, accessibility, and transparency in opening up investment opportunities to a wider audience.

"Our embrace of crowdfunding and digital investor engagement platforms is not just about raising capital—it's about democratizing investment and giving individuals the opportunity to become stakeholders in our success," Emma explained, her eyes scanning the room. "We need to leverage digital platforms such as crowdfunding websites and online investment portals to reach a broader audience of investors, allowing them to contribute to our growth and share in our success."

As she spoke, Emma could see the directors nodding in agreement, their expressions reflecting a growing recognition of the transformative potential of crowdfunding and digital investor engagement. They understood that by embracing digital channels, the company could tap into a new source of capital and build a community of engaged stakeholders.

"But crowdfunding and digital investor engagement require more than just technological infrastructure—they require a commitment to transparency, accountability, and investor education," Emma continued, her voice growing more serious. "We need to ensure that our crowdfunding campaigns are transparent about our business objectives, financial performance, and risks, while also providing investors with clear information and opportunities to engage with us on our journey."

She then outlined strategies for implementing crowdfunding and digital investor engagement, from launching targeted crowdfunding campaigns to hosting virtual investor forums and webinars.

"As leaders, it's our responsibility to ensure that our investment opportunities are accessible, transparent, and inclusive," Emma declared, her tone unwavering. "By prioritizing crowdfunding and digital investor engagement, we can broaden our investor base, unlock new sources of capital, and fuel our growth and innovation in the digital age."

As the discussion unfolded, Emma could sense a palpable determination in the room. The directors, once focused solely on traditional fundraising methods, were now embracing the opportunities of crowdfunding and digital investor engagement, recognizing them as essential to their role in shaping the future of GlobalTech Enterprises.

"With a commitment to crowdfunding and digital investor engagement, we can democratize investment and foster a culture of innovation and collaboration with our stakeholders," Emma concluded, her voice filled with optimism. "Let's embrace this opportunity to lead with empathy, innovation, and integrity, and build a future where everyone has the opportunity to participate in our success."

Harnessing Big Data for Investor Insights

As the dialogue continued within the boardroom, Emma shifted the discussion to another pivotal aspect of their digital governance strategy: harnessing big data for investor insights. She recognized that in the digital age, data-driven decision-making was paramount, and leveraging big data could provide invaluable insights into investor behavior and preferences.

"Ladies and gentlemen, as we delve deeper into our digital governance journey, let us explore the transformative potential of harnessing big data for investor insights," Emma began, her voice filled with anticipation. "In today's data-driven landscape, where information is abundant and insights are currency, we must leverage big data analytics to gain a deeper understanding of investor behavior and preferences."

She guided her directors through an exploration of the importance of harnessing big data, emphasizing the need for agility, foresight, and innovation in leveraging data to inform investor engagement strategies.

"Our embrace of big data analytics is not just about collecting data—it's about extracting meaningful insights that can inform our investor engagement strategies and drive value for our stakeholders," Emma explained, her eyes focused on the attentive faces in the room. "We need to leverage advanced analytics tools and techniques to analyze vast amounts of data from various sources, including market trends, investor sentiment, and demographic profiles, to gain actionable insights into investor behavior and preferences."

As she spoke, Emma could see the directors nodding in agreement, their expressions reflecting a growing recognition of the transformative potential of big data analytics. They understood that by harnessing big data, the company could gain a competitive edge in understanding and responding to investor needs.

"But harnessing big data for investor insights requires more than just technological capability—it requires a culture of data-driven decision-making, privacy protection, and ethical use of data," Emma continued, her voice growing more serious. "We need to ensure that our data collection and analysis processes are compliant with regulatory requirements and respect investor privacy, while also safeguarding against potential biases and ensuring the integrity and accuracy of our insights."

She then outlined strategies for implementing big data analytics for investor insights, from investing in data analytics platforms to training employees on data literacy and ethical data practices.

"As leaders, it's our responsibility to ensure that our investor engagement strategies are informed by data-driven insights and grounded in transparency, accountability, and integrity," Emma declared, her tone unwavering. "By prioritizing the harnessing of big data for investor insights, we can strengthen our relationships with investors, drive value for our company and stakeholders, and position ourselves for long-term success in the digital age."

As the discussion unfolded, Emma could sense a palpable determination in the room. The directors, once focused solely on traditional methods of investor engagement, were now embracing the opportunities of big data analytics, recognizing them as essential to their role in shaping the future of GlobalTech Enterprises.

"With a commitment to harnessing big data for investor insights, we can unlock new opportunities for growth and innovation, and build stronger relationships with our investors in the digital age," Emma concluded, her voice filled with optimism. "Let's embrace this opportunity to lead with foresight, agility, and innovation, and create a future where data-driven decision-making is the cornerstone of our governance practices."

Addressing Shareholder Activism in the Digital Era

As the discussion in the boardroom evolved, Emma redirected the focus towards a critical subpoint of their digital governance strategy: addressing shareholder activism in the digital era. She understood that in today's interconnected world, shareholder activism was on the rise, and embracing digital tools and strategies was essential for effectively managing and responding to shareholder concerns.

"Ladies and gentlemen, as we navigate the complexities of digital governance, let us turn our attention to the pressing issue of addressing shareholder activism in the digital era," Emma began, her voice tinged with urgency. "In an age where social media and digital communication channels empower shareholders to voice their concerns and mobilize support like never before, we must be proactive in our approach to managing shareholder activism and safeguarding the interests of our company and stakeholders."

She guided her directors through an exploration of the challenges posed by shareholder activism in the digital era, emphasizing the need for transparency, responsiveness, and strategic communication in addressing shareholder concerns.

"Our response to shareholder activism cannot be reactive—it must be proactive and rooted in a deep understanding of shareholder concerns and motivations," Emma explained, her eyes scanning the room. "We need to leverage digital communication channels such as social media, investor forums, and online shareholder platforms to engage with shareholders, listen to their concerns, and communicate our perspectives and plans for addressing them."

As she spoke, Emma could see the directors nodding in agreement, their expressions reflecting a growing recognition of the importance of proactive engagement with shareholders. They understood that by embracing digital tools and strategies, the company could effectively manage shareholder activism and maintain trust and confidence in its governance practices.

"But addressing shareholder activism in the digital era requires more than just digital communication—it also requires a culture of openness, accountability, and responsiveness," Emma continued, her voice growing more serious. "We need to ensure that our governance processes are transparent, our decision-making is inclusive, and our responses to shareholder concerns are timely and meaningful."

She then outlined strategies for effectively addressing shareholder activism in the digital era, from establishing clear channels of communication to implementing mechanisms for shareholder engagement and feedback.

"As leaders, it's our responsibility to embrace shareholder activism as an opportunity for dialogue, engagement, and improvement," Emma declared, her tone unwavering. "By prioritizing proactive engagement and strategic communication, we can build stronger relationships with our shareholders, mitigate the risks of activism, and create value for our company and stakeholders."

As the discussion unfolded, Emma could sense a palpable determination in the room. The directors, once wary of shareholder activism, were now embracing the opportunities of proactive engagement, recognizing it as essential to their role in safeguarding the future of GlobalTech Enterprises.

"With a commitment to addressing shareholder activism in the digital era, we can turn challenges into opportunities and build a future where governance is transparent, inclusive, and responsive to the needs of all stakeholders," Emma concluded, her voice filled with optimism. "Let's embrace this opportunity to lead with integrity, empathy, and innovation, and shape a future where shareholder activism is met with understanding, collaboration, and constructive dialogue."

8

Chapter Eight: Digital Governance in Mergers and Acquisitions

"Navigating Digital M&A: Transforming Governance in the Era of Consolidation"

In the expansive boardroom of GlobalTech Enterprises, the atmosphere buzzed with anticipation as Emma Carter, the CEO, prepared to lead her directors through the complexities of digital governance in mergers and acquisitions. With the company eyeing strategic growth opportunities through consolidation, Emma knew that adapting governance practices to the digital age was crucial for ensuring the success of future M&A endeavors.

"Ladies and gentlemen, welcome to a pivotal discussion on digital governance in mergers and acquisitions," Emma began, her voice commanding attention. "As we explore opportunities for strategic growth and expansion, it's imperative that we adapt our governance practices to the realities of the digital era, ensuring alignment, transparency, and accountability throughout the M&A process."

She guided her directors through an exploration of the challenges and opportunities posed by digital governance in M&A, emphasizing the need for agility, foresight, and strategic alignment in navigating the complexities of consolidation in the digital age.

"Our approach to digital governance in M&A must be proactive, collaborative, and forward-thinking," Emma explained, her eyes scanning the room. "We need to leverage digital tools and technologies to streamline due diligence, enhance communication and collaboration with stakeholders, and mitigate risks associated with integration and cultural alignment."

As she spoke, Emma could see the directors nodding in agreement, their expressions reflecting a growing recognition of the importance of digital governance in M&A. They understood that by embracing digital transformation, the company could position itself for success in an increasingly competitive and dynamic market.

"But digital governance in M&A is not without its challenges—it requires careful planning, robust risk management, and a commitment to transparency and integrity," Emma continued, her voice growing more serious. "We need to ensure that our governance structures and processes are adaptable to the unique complexities of M&A transactions, while also upholding our values and responsibilities to our stakeholders."

She then outlined strategies for enhancing digital governance in M&A, from establishing cross-functional integration teams to implementing data-driven decision-making frameworks and leveraging digital platforms for post-merger integration.

"As leaders, it's our responsibility to ensure that our M&A endeavors are guided by principles of transparency, accountability, and responsible stewardship," Emma declared, her tone unwavering. "By prioritizing digital governance in M&A, we can navigate the complexities of consolidation with confidence, create value for our company and stakeholders, and position ourselves for sustainable growth and success in the digital age."

As the discussion unfolded, Emma could sense a palpable determination in the room. The directors, once daunted by the prospect of M&A, were now embracing the opportunities of digital governance, recognizing it as essential to their role in shaping the future of GlobalTech Enterprises.

"With a commitment to digital governance in M&A, we can transform challenges into opportunities and chart a course towards a future of strategic growth and innovation," Emma concluded, her voice filled with optimism. "Let's embrace this opportunity to lead with agility, collaboration, and foresight, and build a future where governance drives value and excellence in every aspect of our operations."

Due Diligence in the Digital Age

In the boardroom, the focus shifted to the critical subpoint of due diligence in the digital age as Emma continued to guide her directors through the intricacies of digital governance in mergers and acquisitions.

"Ladies and gentlemen, let us now delve into the crucial aspect of due diligence in the digital age," Emma began, her voice resonating with authority. "As we embark on

M&A endeavors, it's essential that we conduct thorough due diligence to assess risks, uncover opportunities, and ensure strategic alignment with our goals."

She led her directors through an exploration of the challenges and opportunities presented by due diligence in the digital age, emphasizing the need for comprehensive analysis, agility, and foresight in evaluating potential targets and assessing their digital capabilities and vulnerabilities.

"Our approach to due diligence must evolve to encompass the complexities of the digital landscape," Emma explained, her eyes scanning the room. "We need to leverage data analytics, cybersecurity assessments, and digital audits to gain a comprehensive understanding of the target company's digital infrastructure, systems, and practices."

As she spoke, Emma could see the directors nodding in agreement, their expressions reflecting a growing recognition of the importance of due diligence in M&A. They understood that by embracing digital tools and methodologies, the company could mitigate risks and maximize value in its M&A transactions.

"But due diligence in the digital age requires more than just technological expertise—it also demands collaboration, strategic insight, and a commitment to ethical conduct," Emma continued, her voice growing more serious. "We need to ensure that our due diligence processes are guided by principles of transparency, integrity, and responsible stewardship, while also respecting the confidentiality and privacy of sensitive information."

She then outlined strategies for enhancing due diligence in the digital age, from assembling multidisciplinary due diligence teams to integrating digital expertise into the assessment process and leveraging external partners for specialized insights.

"As leaders, it's our responsibility to ensure that our due diligence efforts are rigorous, thorough, and forward-thinking," Emma declared, her tone unwavering. "By prioritizing due diligence in the digital age, we can minimize risks, uncover hidden opportunities, and make informed decisions that drive value for our company and stakeholders."

As the discussion unfolded, Emma could sense a palpable determination in the room. The directors, once daunted by the complexities of due diligence, were now embracing the opportunities of digital governance, recognizing it as essential to their role in shaping the future of GlobalTech Enterprises.

"With a commitment to due diligence in the digital age, we can navigate the complexities of M&A with confidence and clarity, ensuring the success of our strategic growth initiatives," Emma concluded, her voice filled with optimism. "Let's embrace this opportunity to lead with insight, integrity, and innovation, and build a future where governance drives excellence and value in every aspect of our operations."

Assessing Technology Risks and Opportunities in M&A

In the boardroom of GlobalTech Enterprises, the discussion continued to delve into the intricate details of digital governance in mergers and acquisitions, with Emma leading the charge. This time, the spotlight was on the critical subpoint of assessing technology risks and opportunities in M&A transactions.

"Ladies and gentlemen, let us now turn our attention to the crucial task of assessing technology risks and opportunities in M&A," Emma began, her voice carrying a sense of urgency. "As we navigate the digital landscape, it's imperative that we conduct thorough assessments to understand the technological capabilities and vulnerabilities of potential targets."

She guided her directors through an exploration of the challenges and opportunities presented by assessing technology risks and opportunities, emphasizing the need for strategic insight, foresight, and collaboration in evaluating the technological landscape of target companies.

"Our approach to assessing technology risks and opportunities must be comprehensive and forward-thinking," Emma explained, her eyes meeting the gaze of each director in the room. "We need to conduct deep dives into the target company's technology infrastructure, systems, and processes to identify potential risks, such as cybersecurity vulnerabilities, data privacy concerns, and technological obsolescence."

As she spoke, Emma could see the directors nodding in agreement, their expressions reflecting a growing recognition of the importance of technology assessment in M&A. They understood that by embracing digital tools and methodologies, the company could mitigate risks and capitalize on technological strengths in its M&A transactions.

"But assessing technology risks and opportunities goes beyond mere risk mitigation—it also presents opportunities for innovation, synergies, and growth," Emma continued, her voice growing more serious. "We need to identify areas where technology can drive value creation, such as through digital transformation initiatives, integration of complementary technologies, and leveraging digital assets for competitive advantage."

She then outlined strategies for effectively assessing technology risks and opportunities in M&A, from conducting technology due diligence to engaging with technical experts and leveraging data analytics for insights.

"As leaders, it's our responsibility to ensure that our assessments of technology risks and opportunities are thorough, insightful, and actionable," Emma declared, her tone unwavering. "By prioritizing technology assessment in M&A, we can navigate the complexities of digital transformation with confidence and clarity, ensuring the success of our strategic growth initiatives."

As the discussion unfolded, Emma could sense a palpable determination in the room. The directors, once overwhelmed by the intricacies of technology assessment, were now embracing the opportunities of digital governance, recognizing it as essential to their role in shaping the future of GlobalTech Enterprises.

"With a commitment to assessing technology risks and opportunities in M&A, we can unlock new avenues for growth and innovation, positioning ourselves as leaders in the digital landscape," Emma concluded, her voice filled with optimism. "Let's embrace this opportunity to lead with insight, integrity, and innovation, and build a future where technology drives excellence and value in every aspect of our operations."

Integration Challenges and Strategies for Success

In the hushed tones of the boardroom, Emma's voice cut through the air, anchoring the discussion onto the next crucial subpoint of their M&A strategy: integration challenges and strategies for success.

"Ladies and gentlemen, as we navigate the complexities of mergers and acquisitions, let us now turn our attention to the critical aspect of integration," Emma began, her tone measured yet determined. "The success of our M&A endeavors hinges not only on identifying the right targets but also on seamlessly integrating them into our organization to realize synergies and drive value."

She guided her directors through an exploration of the challenges and opportunities presented by integration, emphasizing the need for strategic planning, collaboration, and agility in merging cultures, systems, and processes.

"Our approach to integration must be holistic, collaborative, and forward-thinking," Emma explained, her eyes scanning the room. "We need to develop comprehensive integration plans that address cultural alignment, operational integration, and technology consolidation to ensure a smooth transition and minimize disruption to our business operations."

As she spoke, Emma could see the directors nodding in agreement, their expressions reflecting a growing recognition of the importance of integration in M&A. They understood that by embracing integration challenges head-on, the company could unlock synergies and accelerate its growth trajectory.

"But integration is not without its challenges—it requires careful planning, effective communication, and a commitment to transparency and empathy," Emma continued, her voice growing more serious. "We need to anticipate potential roadblocks, such as resistance to change, cultural clashes, and technological complexities, and develop strategies to mitigate risks and overcome obstacles."

She then outlined strategies for successful integration, from appointing dedicated integration teams to fostering open communication channels and conducting regular progress assessments.

"As leaders, it's our responsibility to ensure that our integration efforts are guided by principles of collaboration, empathy, and resilience," Emma declared, her tone unwavering. "By prioritizing integration challenges and strategies for success, we can navigate the complexities of M&A with confidence and clarity, ensuring the seamless integration of acquired entities and the realization of value for our company and stakeholders."

As the discussion unfolded, Emma could sense a palpable determination in the room. The directors, once daunted by the prospect of integration, were now embracing the opportunities of digital governance, recognizing it as essential to their role in shaping the future of GlobalTech Enterprises.

"With a commitment to integration challenges and strategies for success, we can transform challenges into opportunities and build a future where synergy and collaboration drive excellence and value in every aspect of our operations," Emma concluded, her voice filled with optimism. "Let's embrace this opportunity to lead with insight, integrity, and innovation, and create a future where integration is not just a process but a catalyst for growth and success."

Legal and Regulatory Considerations in Digital Transactions

In the boardroom, Emma shifted the focus to another critical subpoint: legal and regulatory considerations in digital transactions. She understood that navigating the legal landscape was paramount in ensuring the success and compliance of their M&A endeavors in the digital age.

"Ladies and gentlemen, as we delve deeper into our M&A strategy, it's essential that we address the legal and regulatory considerations inherent in digital transactions," Emma began, her voice carrying a sense of gravity. "In an era where laws and regulations governing digital transactions are constantly evolving, we must remain vigilant and proactive in our approach to compliance."

She guided her directors through an exploration of the legal and regulatory challenges and opportunities presented by digital transactions, emphasizing the need for thorough due diligence, regulatory compliance, and risk management.

"Our approach to legal and regulatory considerations must be comprehensive, strategic, and adaptive," Emma explained, her eyes scanning the room. "We need to stay abreast of the latest legal developments and regulatory requirements in the jurisdictions where we operate, ensuring that our transactions are compliant with applicable laws and regulations."

As she spoke, Emma could see the directors nodding in agreement, their expressions reflecting a growing recognition of the importance of legal and regulatory compliance in digital transactions. They understood that by prioritizing compliance, the company could mitigate legal risks and safeguard its reputation and operations.

"But legal and regulatory compliance is not just about avoiding risks—it's also about seizing opportunities and building trust with our stakeholders," Emma continued, her voice growing more serious. "We need to adopt a proactive approach to compliance, embedding legal and regulatory considerations into every stage of our M&A process, from due diligence to post-transaction integration."

She then outlined strategies for effectively managing legal and regulatory considerations in digital transactions, from engaging legal experts to conducting comprehensive compliance assessments and implementing robust risk mitigation measures.

"As leaders, it's our responsibility to ensure that our M&A transactions are conducted with the highest standards of legal and regulatory compliance," Emma declared, her tone unwavering. "By prioritizing legal and regulatory considerations, we can navigate the complexities of digital transactions with confidence and integrity, ensuring the success and sustainability of our M&A endeavors."

As the discussion unfolded, Emma could sense a palpable determination in the room. The directors, once daunted by the legal complexities of digital transactions, were now embracing the opportunities of digital governance, recognizing it as essential to their role in shaping the future of GlobalTech Enterprises.

"With a commitment to legal and regulatory compliance, we can build a future where trust, transparency, and integrity underpin every aspect of our operations," Emma concluded, her voice filled with optimism. "Let's embrace this opportunity to lead with diligence, foresight, and responsibility, and create a future where compliance is not just a requirement but a cornerstone of our corporate governance."

Cultural Alignment in Merged Digital Entities

In the boardroom, Emma turned the discussion towards a pivotal subpoint: cultural alignment in merged digital entities. She knew that beyond legalities and regulations, ensuring cohesion and harmony in company cultures was paramount for the success of their M&A endeavors in the digital age.

"Ladies and gentlemen, let us now address the crucial aspect of cultural alignment in merged digital entities," Emma began, her voice poised yet commanding. "As we bring together diverse teams and organizations, it's imperative that we foster a culture of unity, collaboration, and shared values to drive our collective success."

She guided her directors through an exploration of the challenges and opportunities presented by cultural alignment in merged digital entities, emphasizing the need for empathy, communication, and leadership in bridging cultural gaps and fostering integration.

"Our approach to cultural alignment must be inclusive, empathetic, and forward-thinking," Emma explained, her eyes meeting the gaze of each director in the room. "We need to recognize and respect the unique cultures and identities of the organizations we merge with, while also identifying common values and aspirations that can serve as the foundation for our shared culture."

As she spoke, Emma could see the directors nodding in agreement, their expressions reflecting a growing recognition of the importance of cultural alignment in M&A. They understood that by prioritizing cultural integration, the company could unlock synergies and maximize the potential of its combined workforce.

"But cultural alignment is not without its challenges—it requires patience, understanding, and a commitment to building trust and camaraderie among team members," Emma continued, her voice growing more serious. "We need to facilitate open and honest communication, provide opportunities for team-building and collaboration, and lead by example in embodying the values and principles of our shared culture."

She then outlined strategies for fostering cultural alignment in merged digital entities, from conducting cultural assessments to implementing cultural integration programs and initiatives.

"As leaders, it's our responsibility to ensure that our merged entities are united by a strong and cohesive culture that reflects our shared vision and values," Emma declared, her tone unwavering. "By prioritizing cultural alignment, we can harness the collective strength and creativity of our diverse teams, driving innovation, and success in the digital age."

As the discussion unfolded, Emma could sense a palpable determination in the room. The directors, once concerned about cultural differences, were now embracing the opportunities of digital governance, recognizing it as essential to their role in shaping the future of GlobalTech Enterprises.

"With a commitment to cultural alignment, we can create a future where diversity is celebrated, collaboration is valued, and success is shared among all members of our merged digital entities," Emma concluded, her voice filled with optimism. "Let's embrace this opportunity to lead with empathy, integrity, and inclusivity, and build a future where our collective strength knows no bounds."

Case Studies: M&A Deals Shaped by Digital Governance

In the boardroom of GlobalTech Enterprises, Emma introduced a compelling subpoint: case studies of M&A deals shaped by digital governance. She knew that real-world examples would provide valuable insights into the practical application of digital governance principles in mergers and acquisitions.

CHAPTER EIGHT: DIGITAL GOVERNANCE IN MERGERS AND...

"Ladies and gentlemen, let us now delve into case studies of M&A deals that have been shaped by digital governance," Emma began, her voice carrying a tone of anticipation. "By examining real-world examples, we can gain valuable insights into the strategies and best practices that have led to successful outcomes in the digital age."

She guided her directors through an exploration of notable M&A deals, highlighting how digital governance principles had influenced their success. From strategic alignment to cultural integration, each case study provided valuable lessons and inspiration for their own M&A endeavors.

"Our approach to M&A can be informed and inspired by the experiences of companies that have successfully navigated the complexities of digital governance," Emma explained, her eyes scanning the room. "By studying these case studies, we can identify patterns, strategies, and pitfalls to avoid, ensuring that our own M&A transactions are guided by the principles of digital governance."

As she spoke, Emma could see the directors leaning forward with interest, their expressions reflecting a genuine curiosity and eagerness to learn from real-world examples. They understood that by studying the successes and failures of others, they could glean valuable insights that would inform their own decision-making processes.

"But these case studies are not just about learning from the experiences of others—they're also about drawing inspiration and confidence from their successes," Emma continued, her voice growing more impassioned. "They remind us that with strategic planning, effective execution, and a commitment to digital governance, we have the power to shape our own success stories in the digital age."

She then proceeded to dissect each case study, analyzing the key factors that had contributed to its success and extracting valuable lessons that could be applied to their own M&A endeavors.

"As leaders, it's our responsibility to learn from the experiences of others, adapt to changing realities, and embrace the opportunities of the digital age," Emma declared, her tone unwavering. "By studying these case studies and applying the lessons learned, we can navigate the complexities of M&A with confidence and clarity, ensuring the success and sustainability of our strategic growth initiatives."

As the discussion unfolded, Emma could sense a palpable energy in the room. The directors, once overwhelmed by the challenges of digital governance, were now inspired by the potential of real-world examples to inform their decision-making and drive their success in the digital age.

"With a commitment to learning, adaptation, and innovation, we can build a future where M&A transactions are guided by principles of digital governance and driven by the pursuit of excellence," Emma concluded, her voice filled with optimism. "Let's embrace this opportunity to lead with courage, curiosity, and conviction, and create a future where our collective success knows no bounds."

9

Chapter Nine: Digital Boardroom Tools and Technologies

"Navigating the Digital Boardroom: Tools and Technologies for Governance Excellence"

As the directors of GlobalTech Enterprises gathered in the boardroom, Emma Carter, the CEO, stood at the head of the table, ready to guide them through the transformative world of digital boardroom tools and technologies.

"Ladies and gentlemen, welcome to a pivotal discussion on digital boardroom tools and technologies," Emma began, her voice resonating with anticipation. "In today's fast-paced and interconnected world, it's essential that we leverage cutting-edge tools and technologies to enhance our governance practices and drive value for our company and stakeholders."

She led her directors through an exploration of the latest advancements in digital boardroom tools and technologies, highlighting their potential to streamline processes, improve decision-making, and enhance collaboration.

"Our approach to governance must evolve to embrace the opportunities of the digital age," Emma explained, her eyes alight with enthusiasm. "By harnessing the power of digital boardroom tools and technologies, we can unlock new levels of efficiency, transparency, and innovation in our governance practices."

As she spoke, Emma could see the directors nodding in agreement, their expressions reflecting a shared excitement for the possibilities of digital transformation. They understood that by embracing digital tools and technologies, the company could position itself for success in an increasingly competitive and dynamic market.

"But adopting digital boardroom tools and technologies is not without its challenges—it requires investment, training, and a commitment to change," Emma continued, her voice growing more serious. "We need to ensure that our adoption of these technologies is strategic, purposeful, and aligned with our governance objectives."

She then outlined a roadmap for integrating digital boardroom tools and technologies into their governance practices, from selecting the right tools to providing training and support for directors and executives.

"As leaders, it's our responsibility to embrace the opportunities of digital transformation and lead our company into the future with confidence and foresight," Emma declared, her tone unwavering. "By prioritizing digital boardroom tools and technologies, we can empower our directors and executives to make informed decisions, drive innovation, and create value for our company and stakeholders."

As the discussion unfolded, Emma could sense a palpable

energy in the room. The directors, once daunted by the challenges of digital transformation, were now inspired by the potential of digital boardroom tools and technologies to revolutionize their governance practices.

"With a commitment to digital boardroom tools and technologies, we can transform our governance practices and create a future where excellence and innovation are the hallmarks of our boardroom," Emma concluded, her voice filled with optimism. "Let's embrace this opportunity to lead with vision, courage, and conviction, and build a future where our company thrives in the digital age."

Board Portal for Efficient Information Management

In the illuminated boardroom of GlobalTech Enterprises, Emma directed the discussion towards a critical subpoint: the implementation of a board portal for efficient information management.

"Ladies and gentlemen, let us now delve into the transformative potential of a board portal for efficient information management," Emma began, her voice echoing with purpose. "In our digital era, the volume and complexity of information we handle require a streamlined solution that empowers us to make informed decisions swiftly and securely."

She guided her directors through an exploration of the advantages offered by a board portal, emphasizing its ability to centralize documents, facilitate collaboration, and ensure data security.

"Our governance practices demand agility and precision," Emma continued, her gaze sweeping across the room. "A board portal serves as our digital nerve center, providing real-time access to essential documents, insights, and communication channels, thereby enabling us to respond promptly to emerging opportunities and challenges."

As she spoke, Emma observed nods of agreement from the directors, their anticipation palpable. They recognized that embracing a board portal was not just a matter of convenience but a strategic imperative for navigating the complexities of modern governance.

"But the adoption of a board portal requires more than just technological implementation—it necessitates a cultural shift towards digital collaboration and accountability," Emma added, her tone growing earnest. "We must foster a culture where information is shared transparently, collaboration is encouraged, and decision-making is informed by data-driven insights."

She then outlined a roadmap for the successful implementation of a board portal, from selecting the right platform to providing training and support for directors and executives.

"As leaders, it's incumbent upon us to embrace the possibilities afforded by digital innovation and lead our company into a future of enhanced governance efficiency and effectiveness," Emma declared, her conviction unwavering. "By prioritizing the implementation of a board portal, we can equip ourselves with the tools necessary to navigate the complexities of our digital landscape with confidence and clarity."

As the discussion progressed, Emma sensed a growing enthusiasm among the directors. The prospect of a board portal resonated with them as a symbol of progress and efficiency, propelling them towards a future where governance excellence was within reach.

"With a commitment to embracing a board portal, we can

unlock new levels of efficiency and collaboration in our governance practices, paving the way for sustained success and innovation," Emma concluded, her voice infused with optimism. "Let's seize this opportunity to lead with vision and purpose, and build a future where our company thrives at the forefront of digital governance."

Virtual Meeting Platforms and Remote Collaboration Tools

In the state-of-the-art boardroom of GlobalTech Enterprises, Emma steered the conversation towards another vital subpoint: the integration of virtual meeting platforms and remote collaboration tools.

"Ladies and gentlemen, let us now explore the transformative potential of virtual meeting platforms and remote collaboration tools," Emma began, her voice resonating with authority. "In today's digital landscape, where remote work has become the new norm, these tools offer us the opportunity to connect, collaborate, and make decisions regardless of our physical location."

She guided her directors through an exploration of the benefits offered by virtual meeting platforms and remote collaboration tools, emphasizing their ability to bridge geographical distances, streamline communication, and foster real-time collaboration.

"Our governance practices demand flexibility and adaptability," Emma continued, her eyes meeting the gaze of each director in the room. "Virtual meeting platforms and remote collaboration tools serve as our digital bridge, enabling us to convene, deliberate, and decide with the same level of efficiency and effectiveness as if we were in the same room."

As she spoke, Emma could see the directors nodding in agreement, their expressions reflecting a recognition of the importance of embracing digital collaboration tools in today's business landscape. They understood that these tools were not just conveniences but essential components of modern governance.

"But the adoption of virtual meeting platforms and remote collaboration tools requires more than just technological proficiency—it demands a cultural shift towards digital collaboration and inclusivity," Emma added, her tone growing more serious. "We must ensure that all directors and stakeholders are equipped with the necessary skills and resources to fully leverage these tools for effective decision-making and collaboration."

She then outlined a roadmap for the successful integration of virtual meeting platforms and remote collaboration tools into their governance practices, from selecting the right platforms to providing training and support for directors and executives.

"As leaders, it's incumbent upon us to embrace the opportunities afforded by digital innovation and lead our company into a future of enhanced collaboration and connectivity," Emma declared, her conviction unwavering. "By prioritizing the integration of virtual meeting platforms and remote collaboration tools, we can overcome geographical barriers, drive productivity, and ensure that our governance practices remain agile and responsive in an increasingly interconnected world."

As the discussion unfolded, Emma sensed a growing enthusiasm among the directors. The prospect of embracing virtual meeting platforms and remote collaboration tools resonated with them as a means to enhance their effectiveness and adaptability in the digital age.

"With a commitment to embracing virtual meeting platforms and remote collaboration tools, we can unlock new levels of collaboration and connectivity in our governance practices, empowering us to lead with confidence and agility in the digital era," Emma concluded, her voice filled with optimism. "Let's seize this opportunity to embrace digital transformation and build a future where our company thrives at the forefront of modern governance."

AI-Powered Analytics for Board Decision-Making

In the sleek confines of the boardroom at GlobalTech Enterprises, Emma Carter pivoted the conversation towards an integral subpoint: the integration of AI-powered analytics for board decision-making.

"Ladies and gentlemen, let us now delve into the realm of AI-powered analytics for board decision-making," Emma began, her voice carrying an air of anticipation. "In our data-rich environment, where insights are paramount to informed decision-making, leveraging AI-powered analytics offers us the opportunity to unlock valuable insights and drive strategic outcomes."

She guided her directors through an exploration of the benefits offered by AI-powered analytics, emphasizing its ability to process vast amounts of data, uncover patterns, and generate predictive insights to inform board deliberations.

"Our governance practices demand informed decision-making and foresight," Emma continued, her gaze sweeping across the room. "AI-powered analytics serves as our digital oracle, providing us with actionable insights and foresight to anticipate trends, identify risks, and seize opportunities in our dynamic business landscape."

As she spoke, Emma observed nods of agreement from the directors, their interest piqued by the potential of AI-driven insights to augment their decision-making processes. They recognized that leveraging AI-powered analytics was not just a luxury but a strategic imperative for staying ahead in an increasingly competitive market.

"But the integration of AI-powered analytics requires more than just technological implementation—it necessitates a cultural shift towards data-driven decision-making and innovation," Emma added, her tone growing more earnest. "We must foster a culture where data is valued as a strategic asset, and where AI-driven insights are embraced as catalysts for informed decision-making and continuous improvement."

She then outlined a roadmap for the successful integration of AI-powered analytics into their governance practices, from selecting the right analytics platforms to fostering a data-driven culture among directors and executives.

"As leaders, it's incumbent upon us to harness the power of AI-driven analytics and lead our company into a future of informed decision-making and strategic foresight," Emma declared, her conviction unwavering. "By prioritizing the integration of AI-powered analytics, we can unlock new levels of intelligence and agility in our governance practices, empowering us to navigate the complexities of our digital landscape with confidence and clarity."

As the discussion progressed, Emma sensed a growing enthusiasm among the directors. The prospect of leveraging AI-powered analytics resonated with them as a means to augment their expertise and drive strategic outcomes with precision.

"With a commitment to embracing AI-powered analytics, we can transform our governance practices and create a future where intelligence and innovation are the cornerstones of our decision-making processes," Emma concluded, her voice infused with optimism. "Let's seize this opportunity to lead with vision and foresight, and build a future where our company thrives at the intersection of human expertise and artificial intelligence."

Digital Dashboards for Real-Time Performance Monitoring

In the bustling confines of the boardroom at GlobalTech Enterprises, Emma Carter shifted the focus towards another vital subpoint: the integration of digital dashboards for real-time performance monitoring.

"Ladies and gentlemen, let us now explore the transformative potential of digital dashboards for real-time performance monitoring," Emma began, her voice infused with purpose. "In our fast-paced business environment, where agility and responsiveness are paramount, leveraging digital dashboards offers us the opportunity to monitor key metrics and track performance in real-time."

She guided her directors through an exploration of the benefits offered by digital dashboards, emphasizing their ability to provide instant access to critical data, visualize trends, and facilitate data-driven decision-making.

"Our governance practices demand visibility and accountability," Emma continued, her eyes scanning the room. "Digital dashboards serve as our digital command center, empowering us to monitor performance metrics, identify emerging trends, and make informed decisions on the fly."

As she spoke, Emma could see the directors nodding in agreement, their expressions reflecting a growing recognition of the importance of real-time performance monitoring in today's business landscape. They understood that digital dashboards were not just tools but essential components of modern governance.

"But the integration of digital dashboards requires more than just technological implementation—it necessitates a cultural shift towards data-driven decision-making and accountability," Emma added, her tone growing more earnest. "We must foster a culture where data is valued as a strategic asset, and where performance metrics are embraced as drivers of continuous improvement and excellence."

She then outlined a roadmap for the successful integration of digital dashboards into their governance practices, from selecting the right dashboard platforms to fostering a culture of data-driven decision-making among directors and executives.

"As leaders, it's incumbent upon us to harness the power of digital dashboards and lead our company into a future of transparency and accountability," Emma declared, her conviction unwavering. "By prioritizing the integration of digital dashboards, we can unlock new levels of visibility and responsiveness in our governance practices, empowering us to drive performance and achieve our strategic objectives with confidence and clarity."

As the discussion unfolded, Emma sensed a palpable energy in the room. The directors, once daunted by the challenges of real-time performance monitoring, were now inspired by the potential of digital dashboards to enhance their governance practices and drive strategic outcomes.

"With a commitment to embracing digital dashboards, we can transform our governance practices and create a future where transparency and accountability are the hallmarks of our decision-making processes," Emma concluded, her voice filled with optimism. "Let's seize this opportunity to lead with vision and purpose, and build a future where our company thrives at the forefront of modern governance."

Secure Communication Channels for Board Discussions

In the hushed ambiance of the GlobalTech Enterprises boardroom, Emma Carter transitioned the dialogue to an essential subpoint: the implementation of secure communication channels for board discussions.

"Ladies and gentlemen, let us now delve into the paramount importance of secure communication channels for board discussions," Emma began, her voice commanding attention. "In an era where data breaches and cybersecurity threats loom large, safeguarding our communications is imperative to protect our company's sensitive information and uphold the trust of our stakeholders."

She guided her directors through an exploration of the critical role played by secure communication channels, underscoring their significance in ensuring confidentiality, integrity, and authenticity in board deliberations.

"Our governance practices demand the highest standards of confidentiality and security," Emma continued, her gaze sweeping across the room. "Secure communication channels serve as our digital fortress, providing encrypted channels for sensitive discussions, protecting against eavesdropping and unauthorized access."

As she spoke, Emma noticed the directors nodding in agreement, their expressions reflecting a shared understanding of the gravity of cybersecurity threats in today's digital landscape. They recognized that secure communication channels were not just a precaution but an essential safeguard for the company's reputation and operations.

"But the implementation of secure communication channels requires more than just technological solutions—it necessitates a cultural shift towards cybersecurity awareness and vigilance," Emma added, her tone growing more resolute. "We must foster a culture where cybersecurity is everyone's responsibility, and where proactive measures are taken to mitigate risks and protect our digital assets."

She then outlined a roadmap for the successful implementation of secure communication channels, from deploying encrypted messaging platforms to providing training and awareness programs for directors and executives.

"As leaders, it's incumbent upon us to prioritize cybersecurity and lead by example in safeguarding our company's communications," Emma declared, her conviction unwavering. "By prioritizing the implementation of secure communication channels, we can fortify our defenses against cyber threats and ensure the confidentiality and integrity of our board discussions."

As the discussion progressed, Emma sensed a growing determination among the directors. The prospect of implementing secure communication channels resonated with them as a proactive measure to protect the company's interests and uphold its reputation.

"With a commitment to embracing secure communication channels, we can fortify our governance practices and create a future where confidentiality and integrity are the cornerstones of our board discussions," Emma concluded, her voice filled with assurance. "Let's seize this opportunity to lead with resilience and vigilance, and build a future where our company thrives in the face of digital threats."

10

Chapter Ten: Governance in the Era of Artificial Intelligence

"Navigating the AI Frontier: Governance in the Era of Artificial Intelligence"

In the boardroom of GlobalTech Enterprises, anticipation crackled in the air as Emma Carter, the CEO, prepared to embark on a pivotal discussion: governance in the era of artificial intelligence.

"Ladies and gentlemen, welcome to a transformative dialogue on governance in the era of artificial intelligence," Emma began, her voice carrying a sense of reverence for the topic at hand. "As we stand on the precipice of a new technological frontier, where the capabilities of artificial intelligence are reshaping industries and societies, it is essential that we explore the implications for governance and leadership."

She guided her directors through an exploration of the profound impact of artificial intelligence on governance practices, highlighting its potential to revolutionize decision-making, enhance efficiency, and drive innovation.

"Our governance practices demand adaptability and foresight," Emma continued, her eyes alight with fervor. "Artificial intelligence represents not just a tool but a paradigm shift—a shift towards data-driven decision-making, predictive analytics, and autonomous systems that have the power to transform how we govern and lead."

As she spoke, Emma could see the directors leaning forward with rapt attention, their minds abuzz with the possibilities and challenges presented by the advent of artificial intelligence. They understood that embracing AI was not just an option but a necessity for staying competitive and relevant in the digital age.

"But the integration of artificial intelligence into our governance practices requires more than just technological proficiency—it demands a cultural shift towards embracing AI as a strategic enabler," Emma added, her tone growing more earnest. "We must foster a culture where AI is viewed as a partner in decision-making, augmenting human expertise and intuition with data-driven insights and predictive analytics."

She then outlined a roadmap for navigating the AI frontier in governance, from implementing AI-powered analytics to fostering a culture of experimentation and learning among directors and executives.

"As leaders, it's incumbent upon us to embrace the opportunities afforded by artificial intelligence and lead our company into a future of data-driven governance and leadership," Emma declared, her conviction unwavering. "By prioritizing the integration of artificial intelligence, we can unlock new levels of efficiency, innovation, and strategic foresight in our governance practices, empowering us to navigate the complexities of the digital landscape with confidence and clarity."

As the discussion unfolded, Emma sensed a palpable energy in the room. The directors, once apprehensive about the implications of AI, were now inspired by the potential to leverage artificial intelligence as a catalyst for transformation and growth.

"With a commitment to embracing artificial intelligence, we can redefine governance and leadership in the digital age, creating a future where data-driven insights and predictive analytics guide our decisions and drive our success," Emma concluded, her voice filled with optimism. "Let's seize this opportunity to lead with vision and courage, and build a future where our company thrives at the forefront of innovation and excellence."

Understanding AI's Impact on Corporate Governance

In the hushed confines of the GlobalTech Enterprises boardroom, Emma Carter transitioned the discussion towards a pivotal subpoint: understanding AI's impact on corporate governance.

"Ladies and gentlemen, let us now delve deeper into understanding AI's profound impact on corporate governance," Emma began, her voice infused with a sense of urgency. "As we navigate the complexities of the digital age, it's crucial that we grasp the transformative power of artificial intelligence and its implications for our governance practices."

She guided her directors through an exploration of the multifaceted ways in which AI was reshaping corporate governance, emphasizing its potential to enhance decision-making, optimize processes, and mitigate risks.

"Our governance landscape is undergoing a seismic shift," Emma continued, her eyes meeting the gaze of each director in the room. "Artificial intelligence offers us the opportunity to harness the power of data and analytics to make more informed decisions, identify emerging trends, and anticipate market shifts with unprecedented accuracy."

As she spoke, Emma observed nods of agreement from the directors, their expressions reflecting a growing awareness of the significance of AI in shaping the future of governance. They understood that AI was not just a technological advancement but a game-changer that would redefine their roles and responsibilities as leaders.

"But with great power comes great responsibility," Emma added, her tone growing more solemn. "As we embrace AI in our governance practices, we must also remain vigilant about its ethical implications, ensuring that our decisions are guided by principles of fairness, transparency, and accountability."

She then outlined a roadmap for understanding AI's impact on corporate governance, from conducting AI readiness assessments to establishing ethical guidelines and governance frameworks for AI-driven decision-making.

"As leaders, it's incumbent upon us to navigate the complexities of AI with wisdom and integrity," Emma declared, her conviction unwavering. "By understanding AI's impact on corporate governance and embracing its potential with prudence and foresight, we can chart a course towards a future where innovation and ethical governance go hand in hand."

As the discussion unfolded, Emma sensed a renewed sense of purpose among the directors. The prospect of leveraging AI to enhance governance practices resonated with them as an opportunity to lead with vision and adaptability in a rapidly evolving landscape.

"With a commitment to understanding AI's impact on corporate governance, we can embrace the future with confidence and clarity, ensuring that our company remains at the forefront of innovation and responsible stewardship," Emma concluded, her voice filled with determination. "Let's seize this opportunity to lead with courage and integrity, and build a future where AI empowers us to achieve our strategic objectives with excellence and integrity."

Ethical and Legal Considerations in AI Adoption

In the dimly lit boardroom of GlobalTech Enterprises, Emma Carter shifted the conversation towards a crucial subpoint: ethical and legal considerations in AI adoption.

"Ladies and gentlemen, let us now delve into the ethical and legal considerations that accompany the adoption of artificial intelligence," Emma began, her voice carrying a weight of responsibility. "As we navigate the frontier of AI, it's imperative that we approach its implementation with a keen awareness of the ethical implications and legal obligations."

She guided her directors through an exploration of the ethical challenges posed by AI, emphasizing the importance of fairness, accountability, and transparency in algorithmic decision-making.

"Our governance practices demand integrity and accountability," Emma continued, her eyes scanning the room. "As we integrate AI into our operations, we must ensure that our algorithms are free from bias, uphold human rights, and respect privacy and data protection regulations."

As she spoke, Emma noticed the directors exchanging concerned glances, their expressions reflecting a growing awareness of the ethical minefield that accompanied AI adoption. They understood that while AI held immense promise, it also posed significant risks if not managed responsibly.

"But beyond ethical considerations, there are also legal obligations that we must fulfill as stewards of AI technology," Emma added, her tone growing more serious. "We must comply with relevant laws and regulations governing data privacy, intellectual property rights, and algorithmic accountability, ensuring that our AI systems operate within legal boundaries."

She then outlined a roadmap for addressing ethical and legal considerations in AI adoption, from conducting ethical impact assessments to establishing robust governance frameworks and compliance mechanisms.

"As leaders, it's incumbent upon us to navigate the ethical and legal complexities of AI with diligence and integrity," Emma declared, her conviction unwavering. "By prioritizing ethical and legal considerations in AI adoption, we can build trust with our stakeholders, mitigate risks, and uphold our commitment to responsible leadership in the digital age."

As the discussion unfolded, Emma sensed a shared commitment among the directors to approach AI adoption with caution and conscientiousness. They recognized that while AI held the potential to revolutionize their operations, it also required careful stewardship to ensure its benefits were realized ethically and responsibly.

"With a commitment to ethical and legal considerations, we can harness the power of AI to drive innovation and create value for our company and stakeholders, while upholding the highest standards of integrity and accountability," Emma concluded, her voice filled with resolve. "Let's seize this opportunity to lead with integrity and foresight, and build a future where AI enhances our governance practices while respecting the rights and dignity of all."

Board Oversight of AI Algorithms and Decision-Making

In the commanding presence of Emma Carter, the GlobalTech Enterprises boardroom buzzed with anticipation as the discussion shifted towards a pivotal subpoint: board oversight of AI algorithms and decision-making.

"Ladies and gentlemen, let us now delve into the crucial role of board oversight in managing AI algorithms and decision-making," Emma began, her voice resonating with authority. "As stewards of this organization, it's incumbent upon us to exercise diligent oversight to ensure that our AI systems operate ethically, responsibly, and in alignment with our strategic objectives."

She guided her directors through an exploration of the importance of board oversight in managing the complexities of AI, emphasizing the need for transparency, accountability, and risk mitigation in algorithmic decision-making processes.

"Our governance practices demand vigilance and accountability," Emma continued, her eyes scanning the room. "As we entrust AI with increasingly consequential decisions, from customer service interactions to strategic planning, it's essential that we establish robust mechanisms for board oversight to safeguard against bias, errors, and unintended consequences."

As she spoke, Emma noticed the directors nodding in agreement, their expressions reflecting a shared understanding of the weighty responsibilities that accompanied AI adoption. They recognized that while AI offered unprecedented opportunities for innovation, it also required careful governance to mitigate risks and ensure ethical outcomes.

"But effective board oversight of AI goes beyond mere scrutiny—it requires active engagement, expertise, and collaboration," Emma added, her tone growing more resolute. "We must cultivate a culture where directors are informed about AI technologies, understand their implications, and actively participate in shaping AI strategies and policies."

She then outlined a roadmap for establishing board oversight of AI algorithms and decision-making, from appointing AI committees to providing directors with ongoing training and education on AI technologies and their implications.

"As leaders, it's incumbent upon us to embrace the opportunities and challenges presented by AI with wisdom and foresight," Emma declared, her conviction unwavering. "By prioritizing board oversight of AI algorithms and decision-making, we can ensure that our AI systems operate with integrity, transparency, and accountability, thereby earning the trust of our stakeholders and fulfilling our fiduciary duties."

As the discussion unfolded, Emma sensed a growing resolve among the directors. The prospect of establishing robust board oversight mechanisms for AI resonated with them as a means to uphold the organization's values and ensure its long-term success in the digital age.

"With a commitment to board oversight of AI algorithms and decision-making, we can navigate the complexities of AI with confidence and integrity, leading our organization towards a future of responsible innovation and sustainable growth," Emma concluded, her voice imbued with conviction. "Let's seize this opportunity to lead with vision and stewardship, and build a future where AI serves as a force for positive change and progress."

Responsible AI Governance Frameworks

In the solemn ambiance of the GlobalTech Enterprises boardroom, Emma Carter, the CEO, steered the conversation towards a pivotal subpoint: responsible AI governance frameworks.

"Ladies and gentlemen, let us now explore the imperative of responsible AI governance frameworks," Emma began, her voice commanding attention. "As we embark on our journey into the realm of artificial intelligence, it is essential that we establish robust frameworks to govern the ethical development, deployment, and use of AI within our organization."

She guided her directors through an exploration of the importance of responsible AI governance frameworks, emphasizing their role in ensuring fairness, transparency, and accountability in AI-driven decision-making processes.

"Our governance practices demand integrity and responsibility," Emma continued, her gaze sweeping across the room. "As we harness the power of AI to drive innovation and efficiency, we must also ensure that our AI systems operate in a manner that aligns with our values, respects human rights, and serves the best interests of society."

As she spoke, Emma observed the directors nodding in agreement, their expressions reflecting a shared commitment to ethical leadership in the adoption and implementation of AI technologies. They understood that while AI held immense promise, it also carried significant risks if not managed responsibly.

"But responsible AI governance is not just a moral imperative—it is also a strategic imperative," Emma added, her tone growing more earnest. "By establishing clear frameworks for ethical AI development, deployment, and monitoring, we can build trust with our stakeholders, mitigate risks, and unlock the full potential of AI to drive value and innovation."

She then outlined a roadmap for developing responsible AI governance frameworks, from conducting ethical impact assessments to establishing AI ethics committees and implementing mechanisms for ongoing monitoring and evaluation.

"As leaders, it's incumbent upon us to lead with integrity and foresight in the adoption and deployment of AI technologies," Emma declared, her conviction unwavering. "By prioritizing responsible AI governance frameworks, we can ensure that our AI systems operate ethically, responsibly, and in alignment with our organizational values, thereby earning the trust and confidence of our stakeholders."

As the discussion unfolded, Emma sensed a palpable determination among the directors. The prospect of developing responsible AI governance frameworks resonated with them as a means to demonstrate leadership in the ethical and responsible use of AI.

"With a commitment to responsible AI governance frameworks, we can chart a course towards a future where AI serves as a force for positive change and progress, enriching lives and driving sustainable growth," Emma concluded, her voice filled with resolve. "Let's seize this opportunity to lead with integrity and responsibility, and build a future where AI enables us to achieve our strategic objectives with excellence and compassion."

AI for Predictive Analytics in Governance Processes

In the focused atmosphere of the GlobalTech Enterprises boardroom, Emma Carter shifted the discussion towards a critical subpoint: the utilization of AI for predictive analytics in governance processes.

"Ladies and gentlemen, let us now delve into the transformative potential of AI for predictive analytics in our governance processes," Emma began, her voice infused with a sense of anticipation. "As we navigate the complexities of the digital age, it's essential that we leverage AI to anticipate trends, identify risks, and make data-driven decisions with precision and foresight."

She guided her directors through an exploration of the benefits offered by AI for predictive analytics, emphasizing its ability to analyze vast amounts of data, detect patterns, and forecast outcomes with unprecedented accuracy.

"Our governance practices demand agility and foresight," Emma continued, her eyes meeting the gaze of each director in the room. "AI-powered predictive analytics enable us to anticipate market shifts, identify emerging risks, and seize opportunities with speed and confidence."

As she spoke, Emma noticed the directors leaning forward with keen interest, their expressions reflecting a growing recognition of the strategic advantages offered by predictive analytics. They understood that while traditional approaches to governance relied on historical data and intuition, AI had the power to revolutionize their decision-making processes by providing real-time insights and predictive capabilities.

"But the adoption of AI for predictive analytics requires more than just technological implementation—it necessitates a cultural shift towards data-driven decision-making and innovation," Emma added, her tone growing more resolute. "We must foster a culture where predictive analytics are embraced as a strategic asset, and where directors and executives are empowered to leverage AI insights to drive value and mitigate risks."

She then outlined a roadmap for integrating AI for predictive analytics into governance processes, from selecting the right AI platforms to providing training and support for directors and executives on interpreting and acting upon AI-generated insights.

"As leaders, it's incumbent upon us to harness the power of AI for predictive analytics and lead our organization into a future of informed decision-making and strategic agility," Emma declared, her conviction unwavering. "By prioritizing the adoption of AI for predictive analytics, we can unlock new levels of efficiency, innovation, and foresight in our governance practices, empowering us to navigate the complexities of the digital landscape with confidence and clarity."

As the discussion unfolded, Emma sensed a palpable excitement in the room. The prospect of leveraging AI for predictive analytics resonated with the directors as a means to stay ahead of the curve and drive strategic outcomes in an increasingly volatile and uncertain environment.

"With a commitment to adopting AI for predictive analytics, we can transform our governance processes and create a future where data-driven insights guide our decisions and drive our success," Emma concluded, her voice filled with optimism. "Let's seize this opportunity to lead with vision and embrace the transformative potential of AI for predictive analytics in governance."

Training and Upskilling for AI-Driven Governance

In the illuminated expanse of the GlobalTech Enterprises boardroom, Emma Carter steered the discussion towards a crucial subpoint: training and upskilling for AI-driven governance.

"Ladies and gentlemen, let us now delve into the imperative of training and upskilling for AI-driven governance," Emma began, her voice resonating with purpose. "As we embrace the transformative power of AI in our governance practices, it's essential that we equip ourselves with the knowledge and skills needed to leverage AI effectively and responsibly."

She guided her directors through an exploration of the importance of training and upskilling, emphasizing the need for continuous learning and adaptation in the face of technological advancements.

"Our governance practices demand agility and expertise," Emma continued, her eyes scanning the room. "As AI becomes increasingly integral to our decision-making processes, it's imperative that we invest in training and upskilling initiatives to ensure that directors and executives have the knowledge and capabilities to leverage AI-driven insights effectively."

As she spoke, Emma observed nods of agreement from the directors, their expressions reflecting a shared recognition of the importance of staying abreast of technological developments. They understood that while AI held immense potential, it also required a commitment to ongoing learning and development to harness its benefits fully.

"But training and upskilling for AI-driven governance is not just about technical proficiency—it's also about fostering a culture of innovation and collaboration," Emma added, her tone growing more impassioned. "We must create opportunities for interdisciplinary learning, where directors and executives from diverse backgrounds come together to exchange insights, share best practices, and collaborate on AI-driven initiatives."

She then outlined a comprehensive training and upskilling program for AI-driven governance, encompassing technical training on AI technologies, data literacy workshops, and leadership development programs focused on fostering a culture of innovation and experimentation.

"As leaders, it's incumbent upon us to invest in our most valuable asset—our people," Emma declared, her conviction unwavering. "By prioritizing training and upskilling for AI-driven governance, we can empower our directors and executives to unlock the full potential of AI, driving innovation, and driving value for our organization and stakeholders."

As the discussion unfolded, Emma sensed a palpable determination among the directors. The prospect of investing in training and upskilling for AI-driven governance resonated with them as a means to stay ahead of the curve and drive organizational success in the digital age.

"With a commitment to training and upskilling, we can cultivate a culture of lifelong learning and innovation, ensuring that our organization remains at the forefront of AI-driven governance," Emma concluded, her voice filled with optimism. "Let's seize this opportunity to lead with vision and invest in our collective future, where knowledge and expertise empower us to navigate the complexities of the digital landscape with confidence and agility."

11

Chapter Eleven: Digital Risk Management and Compliance

"Navigating the Digital Frontier: Risk Management and Compliance in the Digital Age"

In the expansive confines of the GlobalTech Enterprises boardroom, Emma Carter, the CEO, gathered her team to delve into the complexities of digital risk management and compliance.

"Ladies and gentlemen, welcome to a critical discussion on risk management and compliance in the digital age," Emma began, her voice commanding attention. "As we navigate the ever-evolving landscape of technology and data, it's imperative that we prioritize proactive risk management and robust compliance practices to safeguard our organization's reputation and future."

She guided her directors through an exploration of the unique challenges posed by the digital landscape, emphasizing the need for agility, foresight, and resilience in the face of emerging threats and regulatory complexities.

"Our governance practices demand vigilance and adaptability," Emma continued, her eyes meeting the gaze of each director in the room. "As we embrace digital transformation, we must also recognize the inherent risks—from cybersecurity threats to data privacy concerns—that accompany our journey into the digital frontier."

As she spoke, Emma noticed the directors nodding in agreement, their expressions reflecting a shared understanding of the urgency of the challenge. They understood that while digital innovation promised unprecedented opportunities, it also brought new risks that required careful management and mitigation.

"But effective risk management and compliance in the digital age require more than just reactive measures—it necessitates a proactive approach that integrates risk management into our strategic decision-making processes," Emma added, her tone growing more resolute. "We must establish robust frameworks for identifying, assessing, and mitigating digital risks, while also ensuring compliance with a rapidly evolving regulatory landscape."

She then outlined a comprehensive approach to digital risk management and compliance, encompassing risk assessments, cybersecurity measures, data governance frameworks, and regulatory compliance initiatives.

"As leaders, it's incumbent upon us to lead with foresight and integrity in the face of digital risk," Emma declared, her conviction unwavering. "By prioritizing digital risk management and compliance, we can build trust with our stakeholders, protect our organization from harm, and create a future where digital innovation drives sustainable growth and success."

As the discussion unfolded, Emma sensed a shared determination among the directors. The prospect of navigating the digital frontier with confidence and resilience resonated with them as a collective imperative for safeguarding the organization's interests and reputation.

"With a commitment to proactive risk management and robust compliance practices, we can navigate the complexities of the digital landscape with confidence and integrity," Emma concluded, her voice filled with resolve. "Let's seize this opportunity to lead with vision and stewardship, and build a future where digital innovation serves as a catalyst for our organization's continued success and resilience."

Identifying and Assessing Digital Risks

In the commanding presence of Emma Carter, the GlobalTech Enterprises boardroom buzzed with anticipation as the discussion shifted towards a critical subpoint: identifying and assessing digital risks.

"Ladies and gentlemen, let us now delve into the imperative of identifying and assessing digital risks," Emma began, her voice resonating with purpose. "As we navigate the digital landscape, it's essential that we possess a clear understanding of the risks that accompany our digital initiatives, from cybersecurity threats to regulatory compliance challenges."

She guided her directors through an exploration of the multifaceted nature of digital risks, emphasizing the need for a proactive approach to risk identification and assessment.

"Our governance practices demand vigilance and foresight," Emma continued, her eyes scanning the room. "As we embrace

CHAPTER ELEVEN: DIGITAL RISK MANAGEMENT AND COMPLIANCE

digital transformation, we must also recognize the potential risks—from data breaches to regulatory fines—that could impact our organization's operations, reputation, and bottom line."

As she spoke, Emma observed the directors nodding in agreement, their expressions reflecting a shared recognition of the urgency of the task. They understood that while digital innovation promised unprecedented opportunities, it also brought new risks that required careful management and mitigation.

"But identifying and assessing digital risks is not just about recognizing the threats—it's also about understanding their potential impact on our organization and stakeholders," Emma added, her tone growing more resolute. "We must conduct comprehensive risk assessments that take into account the likelihood and severity of potential risks, as well as their potential impact on our strategic objectives and financial performance."

She then outlined a systematic approach to identifying and assessing digital risks, encompassing risk identification workshops, scenario planning exercises, and risk quantification techniques to prioritize risks based on their potential impact.

"As leaders, it's incumbent upon us to lead with diligence and foresight in the face of digital risks," Emma declared, her conviction unwavering. "By prioritizing the identification and assessment of digital risks, we can proactively mitigate threats, protect our organization's interests, and create a future where digital innovation drives sustainable growth and success."

As the discussion unfolded, Emma sensed a palpable determination among the directors. The prospect of navigating the digital landscape with confidence and resilience resonated with them as a collective imperative for safeguarding the organization's interests and reputation.

"With a commitment to identifying and assessing digital risks, we can navigate the complexities of the digital landscape with confidence and integrity," Emma concluded, her voice filled with resolve. "Let's seize this opportunity to lead with vision and stewardship, and build a future where digital innovation serves as a catalyst for our organization's continued success and resilience."

Compliance Challenges in a Digitally Transformed World

In the boardroom of GlobalTech Enterprises, Emma Carter, the CEO, directed the conversation towards a critical subpoint: compliance challenges in a digitally transformed world.

"Ladies and gentlemen, let us now address the significant compliance challenges that accompany our journey into the digitally transformed world," Emma began, her voice carrying a weight of responsibility. "As we embrace digital innovation, we must also navigate a complex regulatory landscape that governs data privacy, cybersecurity, and ethical standards."

She guided her directors through an exploration of the evolving regulatory environment, emphasizing the need for a proactive approach to compliance in the face of rapid technological change.

"Our governance practices demand agility and foresight," Emma continued, her eyes meeting the gaze of each director in the room. "As digital transformation accelerates, so too do the regulatory requirements that govern our operations. From GDPR to CCPA, we must ensure that we comply with relevant laws and regulations to protect our organization's reputation and mitigate legal risks."

As she spoke, Emma noticed the directors exchanging concerned glances, their expressions reflecting a growing awareness of the complexities of regulatory compliance in the digital age. They understood that while digital innovation offered unprecedented opportunities, it also brought new compliance challenges that required careful navigation and adherence.

"But compliance in a digitally transformed world is not just about meeting regulatory requirements—it's also about upholding our ethical principles and societal responsibilities," Emma added, her tone growing more resolute. "We must embed compliance into our organizational culture, ensuring that every decision and action reflects our commitment to integrity, transparency, and accountability."

She then outlined a comprehensive approach to compliance in a digitally transformed world, encompassing regular audits, compliance training programs, and the establishment of cross-functional compliance teams to ensure alignment with regulatory requirements and ethical standards.

"As leaders, it's incumbent upon us to lead with integrity and foresight in the face of compliance challenges," Emma declared, her conviction unwavering. "By prioritizing compliance in a digitally transformed world, we can build trust with our stakeholders, protect our organization from legal and reputational risks, and create a future where digital innovation drives sustainable growth and success."

As the discussion unfolded, Emma sensed a palpable determination among the directors. The prospect of navigating the complex regulatory landscape with confidence and integrity resonated with them as a collective imperative for safeguarding the organization's interests and reputation.

"With a commitment to compliance in a digitally transformed world, we can navigate the complexities of the regulatory landscape with confidence and integrity," Emma concluded, her voice filled with resolve. "Let's seize this opportunity to lead with vision and stewardship, and build a future where digital innovation serves as a catalyst for our organization's continued success and resilience."

Implementing Effective Internal Controls for Digital Operations

In the commanding aura of the GlobalTech Enterprises boardroom, Emma Carter steered the dialogue towards a crucial subpoint: implementing effective internal controls for digital operations.

"Ladies and gentlemen, let us now delve into the imperative of implementing effective internal controls for our digital operations," Emma began, her voice resonating with purpose. "As we navigate the complexities of the digital landscape, it's essential that we establish robust internal controls to safeguard our assets, ensure compliance, and mitigate risks."

She guided her directors through an exploration of the significance of internal controls in the digital realm, emphasizing the need for agility, transparency, and accountability in the face of evolving technological landscapes.

"Our governance practices demand vigilance and adaptability," Emma continued, her eyes scanning the room. "As digital transformation accelerates, so too must our internal controls evolve to address new threats and vulnerabilities, from cyberattacks to data breaches."

As she spoke, Emma observed the directors nodding in agreement, their expressions reflecting a shared understanding of the urgency of the task. They recognized that while digital innovation promised unprecedented opportunities, it also brought new risks that required careful management and mitigation through effective internal controls.

"But implementing effective internal controls for digital operations is not just about implementing technology—it's also about fostering a culture of accountability and responsibility," Emma added, her tone growing more resolute. "We must ensure that our internal controls are aligned with our strategic objectives, and that every employee understands their role in maintaining the integrity and security of our digital assets."

She then outlined a comprehensive approach to implementing internal controls for digital operations, encompassing regular risk assessments, cybersecurity training programs, and the implementation of automated monitoring and reporting systems to detect and respond to anomalies.

"As leaders, it's incumbent upon us to lead with integrity and foresight in the face of digital risks," Emma declared, her conviction unwavering. "By prioritizing the implementation of effective internal controls, we can safeguard our organization's assets, protect our stakeholders' interests, and create a future where digital innovation drives sustainable growth and success."

As the discussion unfolded, Emma sensed a palpable determination among the directors. The prospect of implementing robust internal controls for digital operations resonated with them as a collective imperative for safeguarding the organization's interests and reputation.

"With a commitment to implementing effective internal controls, we can navigate the complexities of the digital landscape with confidence and integrity," Emma concluded, her voice filled with resolve. "Let's seize this opportunity to lead with vision and stewardship, and build a future where digital innovation serves as a catalyst for our organization's continued success and resilience."

Regulatory Compliance in Cloud Computing and Salas Solutions

In the prestigious boardroom of GlobalTech Enterprises, Emma Carter directed the discussion towards a pivotal subpoint: regulatory compliance in cloud computing and SaaS solutions.

"Ladies and gentlemen, let us now turn our attention to the critical aspect of regulatory compliance in our cloud computing and SaaS solutions," Emma began, her voice commanding attention. "As we harness the power of cloud technology to drive innovation and efficiency, we must also ensure that our operations comply with the ever-evolving regulatory landscape."

She guided her directors through an exploration of the challenges and opportunities presented by cloud computing and SaaS solutions, emphasizing the need for proactive compliance measures in the face of complex regulatory requirements.

"Our governance practices demand vigilance and adaptability," Emma continued, her eyes scanning the room. "As we leverage cloud computing and SaaS solutions to transform our operations, we must navigate a myriad of regulatory considerations, from data privacy regulations to industry-specific compliance standards."

As she spoke, Emma observed the directors nodding in

agreement, their expressions reflecting a shared recognition of the importance of regulatory compliance in the digital age. They understood that while cloud technology offered unparalleled scalability and flexibility, it also brought new compliance challenges that required careful navigation and adherence.

"But regulatory compliance in cloud computing and SaaS solutions is not just about meeting legal requirements—it's also about safeguarding our data and protecting our stakeholders' interests," Emma added, her tone growing more resolute. "We must ensure that our cloud providers adhere to stringent security and privacy standards, and that our data is handled with the utmost care and integrity."

She then outlined a comprehensive approach to regulatory compliance in cloud computing and SaaS solutions, encompassing due diligence in vendor selection, regular audits of cloud infrastructure, and the implementation of data governance frameworks to ensure compliance with applicable regulations.

"As leaders, it's incumbent upon us to lead with integrity and foresight in the face of regulatory challenges," Emma declared, her conviction unwavering. "By prioritizing regulatory compliance in cloud computing and SaaS solutions, we can build trust with our stakeholders, protect our organization from legal and reputational risks, and create a future where digital innovation drives sustainable growth and success."

As the discussion unfolded, Emma sensed a palpable determination among the directors. The prospect of ensuring regulatory compliance in cloud computing and SaaS solutions resonated with them as a collective imperative for safeguarding the organization's interests and reputation.

"With a commitment to regulatory compliance, we can navigate the complexities of the digital landscape with confidence and integrity," Emma concluded, her voice filled with resolve. "Let's seize this opportunity to lead with vision and stewardship, and build a future where cloud technology serves as a catalyst for our organization's continued success and resilience."

Auditing Digital Systems and Processes

In the dynamic atmosphere of the GlobalTech Enterprises boardroom, Emma Carter pivoted the discussion towards a crucial subpoint: auditing digital systems and processes.

"Ladies and gentlemen, let us now delve into the vital aspect of auditing our digital systems and processes," Emma began, her voice resonating with authority. "As we embrace digital transformation, it's imperative that we maintain transparency and accountability through regular audits to ensure the integrity and efficiency of our operations."

She guided her directors through an exploration of the significance of auditing digital systems and processes, emphasizing the need for thorough assessments in the face of rapidly evolving technologies and regulatory requirements.

"Our governance practices demand diligence and adaptability," Emma continued, her eyes scanning the room. "As digital innovation reshapes our business landscape, we must conduct comprehensive audits to identify potential risks, assess controls, and verify compliance with internal policies and external regulations."

As she spoke, Emma noticed the directors nodding in agreement, their expressions reflecting a shared understanding of the importance of auditing in the digital age. They recognized that while digital transformation promised enhanced efficiency and agility, it also brought new complexities that necessitated rigorous oversight.

"But auditing digital systems and processes goes beyond mere compliance—it's also about driving continuous improvement and innovation," Emma added, her tone growing more resolute. "We must leverage audit findings to identify areas for optimization, enhance cybersecurity measures, and strengthen governance frameworks to support our organization's strategic objectives."

She then outlined a systematic approach to auditing digital systems and processes, encompassing risk-based audit planning, data analytics for enhanced insights, and collaboration with internal and external stakeholders to drive accountability and transparency.

"As leaders, it's incumbent upon us to lead with integrity and foresight in the face of digital challenges," Emma declared, her conviction unwavering. "By prioritizing audits of our digital systems and processes, we can mitigate risks, enhance operational efficiency, and build trust with our stakeholders, thereby ensuring our organization's continued success and resilience."

As the discussion unfolded, Emma sensed a palpable determination among the directors. The prospect of conducting thorough audits resonated with them as a collective imperative for safeguarding the organization's interests and reputation in the digital age.

"With a commitment to auditing digital systems and processes, we can navigate the complexities of the digital landscape with confidence and integrity," Emma concluded, her voice filled with resolve. "Let's seize this opportunity to lead with vision and stewardship, and build a future where digital innovation serves as a catalyst for our organization's sustained growth and excellence."

Continuous Monitoring and Adaptation to Regulatory Changes

In the prestigious boardroom of GlobalTech Enterprises, Emma Carter steered the conversation towards a pivotal subpoint: continuous monitoring and adaptation to regulatory changes.

"Ladies and gentlemen, let us now address the critical aspect of continuous monitoring and adaptation to regulatory changes," Emma began, her voice carrying authority. "As we operate in an ever-evolving regulatory landscape, it's imperative that we maintain vigilance and agility to ensure compliance with new and changing regulations."

She guided her directors through an exploration of the significance of continuous monitoring and adaptation, emphasizing the need for proactive measures to stay ahead of regulatory developments and mitigate compliance risks.

"Our governance practices demand foresight and adaptability," Emma continued, her eyes meeting the gaze of each director in the room. "As regulatory requirements evolve, so too must our governance frameworks and operational practices. We must be proactive in monitoring regulatory changes and agile in adapting our processes to ensure ongoing compliance."

As she spoke, Emma observed the directors nodding in agreement, their expressions reflecting a shared recognition of the importance of staying abreast of regulatory changes. They understood that while regulatory compliance was essential, it required continuous effort and attention to keep pace with shifting requirements.

"But continuous monitoring and adaptation to regulatory changes is not just about compliance—it's also about maintaining our organization's reputation and competitive advantage," Emma added, her tone growing more resolute. "By staying ahead of regulatory developments, we can demonstrate our commitment to integrity and accountability, thereby building trust with our stakeholders and enhancing our market position."

She then outlined a systematic approach to continuous monitoring and adaptation, encompassing regular reviews of regulatory updates, collaboration with legal and compliance experts, and the implementation of agile processes to quickly adapt to changing requirements.

"As leaders, it's incumbent upon us to lead with integrity and foresight in the face of regulatory challenges," Emma declared, her conviction unwavering. "By prioritizing continuous monitoring and adaptation, we can mitigate compliance risks, protect our organization's interests, and create a future where regulatory compliance is a cornerstone of our success."

As the discussion unfolded, Emma sensed a palpable determination among the directors. The prospect of embracing continuous monitoring and adaptation resonated with them as a collective imperative for safeguarding the organization's interests and reputation in a dynamic regulatory environment.

"With a commitment to continuous monitoring and adaptation, we can navigate the complexities of the regulatory landscape with confidence and integrity," Emma concluded, her voice filled with resolve. "Let's seize this opportunity to lead with vision and stewardship, and build a future where regulatory compliance is a driver of our organization's sustained growth and excellence."

12

Chapter Twelve: Global Governance in a Digitalized World

"Bridging Borders: Global Governance in the Digital Age"

In the expansive boardroom of GlobalTech Enterprises, Emma Carter, the CEO, convened a pivotal discussion on global governance in a digitalized world.

"Ladies and gentlemen, welcome to a crucial conversation on global governance in the digital age," Emma began, her voice commanding attention. "As our operations transcend borders and our reach extends across continents, it's imperative that we navigate the complexities of global governance with diligence and foresight."

She guided her directors through an exploration of the significance of global governance in the digital era, emphasizing the need for a cohesive approach to governance that transcends geographical boundaries.

"Our governance practices demand global perspective and adaptability," Emma continued, her eyes scanning the room.

"As we operate in a digitalized world, we must recognize that regulatory requirements, cultural norms, and business practices vary widely across regions. We must be agile in our approach to governance, ensuring that we adhere to local laws and customs while upholding our global standards of integrity and accountability."

As she spoke, Emma noticed the directors nodding in agreement, their expressions reflecting a shared understanding of the importance of global governance in today's interconnected world. They understood that while digital innovation offered unprecedented opportunities for global expansion, it also brought new challenges that required careful consideration and navigation.

"But global governance in a digitalized world is not just about compliance—it's also about fostering collaboration and trust across borders," Emma added, her tone growing more resolute. "We must build strong relationships with regulators, partners, and stakeholders in every region where we operate, demonstrating our commitment to responsible stewardship and ethical business practices."

She then outlined a comprehensive approach to global governance in a digitalized world, encompassing cultural sensitivity training, cross-border collaboration initiatives, and the establishment of global governance frameworks to ensure consistency and alignment across regions.

"As leaders, it's incumbent upon us to lead with vision and cultural sensitivity in the face of global challenges," Emma declared, her conviction unwavering. "By prioritizing global governance, we can build bridges across borders, foster trust with our stakeholders, and create a future where digital innovation serves as a catalyst for global prosperity and collaboration."

As the discussion unfolded, Emma sensed a palpable determination among the directors. The prospect of embracing global governance resonated with them as a collective imperative for ensuring the organization's success and sustainability in an increasingly interconnected world.

"With a commitment to global governance, we can navigate the complexities of the digitalized world with confidence and integrity," Emma concluded, her voice filled with resolve. "Let's seize this opportunity to lead with vision and stewardship, and build a future where our global footprint reflects our commitment to excellence and responsible leadership."

Understanding AI's Impact on Corporate Governance

In the expansive boardroom of GlobalTech Enterprises, Emma Carter shifted the focus towards a crucial subpoint: understanding AI's impact on corporate governance.

"Ladies and gentlemen, let us now delve into the profound impact of artificial intelligence on corporate governance," Emma began, her voice projecting authority. "As AI continues to revolutionize industries and reshape business landscapes, it's imperative that we grasp its implications for governance practices and strategic decision-making."

She guided her directors through an exploration of the significance of AI in corporate governance, emphasizing the need for a nuanced understanding of its potential benefits and challenges.

"Our governance practices demand adaptability and foresight," Emma continued, her eyes scanning the room. "As AI technologies proliferate, they offer unparalleled opportunities to enhance efficiency, optimize processes, and drive innovation. However, they also introduce new complexities and ethical considerations that require careful consideration."

As she spoke, Emma noticed the directors leaning in with heightened interest, their expressions reflecting a mix of curiosity and concern. They understood that while AI promised transformative benefits, it also raised important questions about transparency, accountability, and the ethical use of data.

"But understanding AI's impact on corporate governance is not just about embracing technology—it's also about embracing a culture of responsible innovation," Emma added, her tone growing more resolute. "We must ensure that our AI systems are designed and deployed in a manner that upholds our values, respects individual privacy, and mitigates biases and unintended consequences."

She then outlined a comprehensive approach to understanding AI's impact on corporate governance, encompassing AI education and training programs for board members, the establishment of AI ethics committees, and the implementation of robust AI governance frameworks to ensure accountability and transparency.

"As leaders, it's incumbent upon us to lead with integrity and foresight in the face of technological disruption," Emma declared, her conviction unwavering. "By prioritizing a deep understanding of AI's impact on corporate governance, we can harness its transformative potential while safeguarding our organization's values and reputation."

As the discussion unfolded, Emma sensed a palpable curiosity and determination among the directors. The prospect of navigating the complexities of AI resonated with them as a collective imperative for ensuring the organization's continued relevance and success in a rapidly evolving digital landscape.

"With a commitment to understanding AI's impact on corporate governance, we can embrace the opportunities of the digital age while remaining true to our core principles," Emma concluded, her voice filled with resolve. "Let's seize this opportunity to lead with vision and integrity, and build a future where AI serves as a force for positive change and responsible stewardship."

Navigating Cross-Border Governance Challenges

In the grandeur of the GlobalTech Enterprises boardroom, Emma Carter pivoted the conversation towards a crucial subpoint: navigating cross-border governance challenges.

"Ladies and gentlemen, let us now address the intricate realm of cross-border governance challenges," Emma began, her voice carrying a tone of gravitas. "As our operations extend across borders and continents, we encounter a multitude of regulatory frameworks, cultural nuances, and geopolitical complexities that demand our attention and strategic foresight."

She guided her directors through an exploration of the significance of cross-border governance challenges, emphasizing the need for a comprehensive understanding of global regulatory environments and cultural sensitivities.

"Our governance practices demand cultural awareness and adaptability," Emma continued, her gaze sweeping across the room. "As we expand our presence globally, we must navigate diverse legal landscapes and cultural norms with diligence and respect. Each jurisdiction presents unique challenges and opportunities that require tailored approaches to governance."

As she spoke, Emma observed the directors nodding thoughtfully, their expressions reflecting a recognition of the intricacies involved in global expansion. They understood that while international markets offered immense potential, they also required careful navigation to ensure compliance and mitigate risks.

"But navigating cross-border governance challenges is not just about compliance—it's also about building trust and fostering relationships across borders," Emma added, her tone growing more resolute. "We must engage with local stakeholders, regulators, and communities in a spirit of collaboration and partnership, demonstrating our commitment to responsible global citizenship and ethical business practices."

She then outlined a comprehensive approach to navigating cross-border governance challenges, encompassing cross-cultural training for employees, the establishment of regional governance committees, and proactive engagement with legal and regulatory experts in each jurisdiction.

"As leaders, it's incumbent upon us to lead with humility and cultural sensitivity in the face of cross-border challenges," Emma declared, her conviction unwavering. "By prioritizing a deep understanding of local contexts and fostering open dialogue across borders, we can build bridges of trust and cooperation, ensuring our organization's success and sustainability in a globalized world."

As the discussion unfolded, Emma sensed a palpable determination and solidarity among the directors. The prospect of navigating cross-border governance challenges resonated with them as a collective imperative for ensuring the organization's continued growth and relevance on the global stage.

"With a commitment to navigating cross-border governance challenges, we can expand our horizons and seize new opportunities with confidence and integrity," Emma concluded, her voice filled with resolve. "Let's embrace the complexities of the global landscape as catalysts for growth and collaboration, and build a future where our organization thrives as a responsible global leader."

Harmonizing Governance Practices Across Different Jurisdictions

In the esteemed GlobalTech Enterprises boardroom, Emma Carter directed the discourse towards a pivotal subpoint: harmonizing governance practices across different jurisdictions.

"Ladies and gentlemen, let us now delve into the intricate task of harmonizing governance practices across diverse jurisdictions," Emma began, her voice echoing with authority. "As our operations span across continents, we face the challenge of reconciling varying regulatory landscapes and cultural norms to uphold our standards of governance excellence."

She steered her directors through an exploration of the significance of harmonizing governance practices, emphasizing the need for consistency and alignment amidst the diversity of global markets.

"Our governance practices demand cohesion and adaptability," Emma continued, her eyes scanning the room. "As we navigate regulatory complexities in different jurisdictions, we must strive for harmonization of our governance frameworks to ensure clarity, transparency, and compliance across the board."

As she spoke, Emma noticed the directors nodding in agreement, their expressions reflecting a shared understanding of the importance of consistency in governance practices. They recognized that while each jurisdiction presented its unique challenges, a unified approach was essential to maintain the organization's integrity and reputation.

"But harmonizing governance practices is not merely a matter of standardization—it's about respecting local laws and customs while upholding our global standards of integrity," Emma added, her tone growing more resolute. "We must strike a balance between centralization and decentralization, empowering local teams to adapt governance frameworks to meet regional needs while ensuring alignment with our overarching principles."

She then outlined a systematic approach to harmonizing governance practices, encompassing regular audits of governance structures, cross-functional collaboration across regions, and the establishment of clear communication channels to disseminate best practices.

"As leaders, it's incumbent upon us to lead with empathy and cultural sensitivity in the pursuit of harmonized governance," Emma declared, her conviction unwavering. "By prioritizing alignment and collaboration, we can navigate the complexities of global markets with integrity and agility, ensuring our organization's sustained success and reputation as a responsible global citizen."

As the discussion unfolded, Emma sensed a palpable resolve and unity among the directors. The prospect of harmonizing governance practices resonated with them as a collective imperative for maintaining the organization's values and fostering trust across borders.

"With a commitment to harmonizing governance practices,

we can navigate the complexities of global markets with confidence and integrity," Emma concluded, her voice filled with conviction. "Let's seize this opportunity to lead with vision and collaboration, and build a future where our governance practices serve as a beacon of excellence and ethical leadership in every corner of the world."

Managing Cultural and Legal Diversity in Global Operations

In the grandeur of the GlobalTech Enterprises boardroom, Emma Carter redirected the discussion towards a pivotal subpoint: managing cultural and legal diversity in global operations.

"Ladies and gentlemen, let us now turn our attention to the multifaceted challenge of managing cultural and legal diversity in our global operations," Emma began, her voice commanding attention. "As we expand our footprint across diverse regions, we encounter a rich tapestry of cultures, traditions, and legal frameworks that demand our utmost attention and respect."

She guided her directors through an exploration of the significance of managing cultural and legal diversity, emphasizing the need for sensitivity and adaptability in navigating the complexities of global markets.

"Our governance practices demand cultural intelligence and legal acumen," Emma continued, her eyes scanning the room. "As we operate in different jurisdictions, we must recognize and respect the unique cultural nuances and legal intricacies that shape business practices and regulatory environments."

As she spoke, Emma noticed the directors nodding in agreement, their expressions reflecting a shared recognition of the importance of cultural and legal diversity in global operations. They understood that while diversity presented opportunities for growth, it also required careful management to avoid misunderstandings and compliance issues.

"But managing cultural and legal diversity is not just about compliance—it's about fostering inclusivity and building bridges across cultures," Emma added, her tone growing more resolute. "We must embrace diversity as a source of strength, leveraging our differences to drive innovation, collaboration, and mutual understanding."

She then outlined a comprehensive approach to managing cultural and legal diversity, encompassing cross-cultural training programs, local legal expertise, and the establishment of diversity and inclusion initiatives to foster a culture of respect and belonging.

"As leaders, it's incumbent upon us to lead with empathy and cultural sensitivity in the face of diversity," Emma declared, her conviction unwavering. "By prioritizing the management of cultural and legal diversity, we can build trust with our stakeholders, mitigate risks, and create a future where diversity is celebrated as a cornerstone of our success."

As the discussion unfolded, Emma sensed a palpable determination and solidarity among the directors. The prospect of managing cultural and legal diversity resonated with them as a collective imperative for ensuring the organization's continued growth and relevance in a globalized world.

"With a commitment to managing cultural and legal diversity, we can navigate the complexities of global operations with confidence and integrity," Emma concluded, her voice filled with resolve. "Let's seize this opportunity to lead with vision and inclusion, and build a future where diversity is not just embraced, but celebrated as a catalyst for innovation and growth."

Digital Governance in Emerging Markets

In the prestigious GlobalTech Enterprises boardroom, Emma Carter steered the conversation towards a crucial subpoint: digital governance in emerging markets.

"Ladies and gentlemen, let us now explore the intricacies of digital governance in emerging markets," Emma began, her voice resonating with authority. "As we expand our presence into these dynamic regions, we encounter unique opportunities and challenges that require a tailored approach to governance."

She guided her directors through an exploration of the significance of digital governance in emerging markets, emphasizing the need for adaptability and innovation in navigating the complexities of rapidly evolving economies.

"Our governance practices demand flexibility and foresight," Emma continued, her eyes scanning the room. "In emerging markets, technological advancements often outpace regulatory frameworks, creating both opportunities for growth and risks for compliance."

As she spoke, Emma noticed the directors leaning in with heightened interest, their expressions reflecting a mix of curiosity and anticipation. They understood that while emerging markets offered immense potential for expansion, they also required a nuanced understanding of local dynamics and regulatory environments.

"But digital governance in emerging markets is not just about compliance—it's also about empowerment and partnership,"

Emma added, her tone growing more resolute. "We must collaborate with local stakeholders, regulators, and communities to co-create governance frameworks that foster innovation, transparency, and inclusive growth."

She then outlined a strategic approach to digital governance in emerging markets, encompassing capacity-building initiatives, cross-sectoral partnerships, and the development of scalable governance models tailored to the needs of each market.

"As leaders, it's incumbent upon us to lead with humility and collaboration in the pursuit of digital governance in emerging markets," Emma declared, her conviction unwavering. "By prioritizing local engagement and innovation, we can unlock the full potential of these vibrant economies while upholding our commitment to responsible stewardship and ethical business practices."

As the discussion unfolded, Emma sensed a palpable determination and excitement among the directors. The prospect of shaping digital governance in emerging markets resonated with them as a collective imperative for driving sustainable growth and impact in these dynamic regions.

"With a commitment to digital governance in emerging markets, we can harness the transformative power of technology to create a future where innovation and prosperity are accessible to all," Emma concluded, her voice filled with resolve. "Let's seize this opportunity to lead with vision and partnership, and build a future where our global impact reflects our values and aspirations for a better world."

International Standards and Best Practices for Digital Governance

In the illustrious boardroom of GlobalTech Enterprises, Emma Carter shifted the conversation towards a pivotal subpoint: international standards and best practices for digital governance.

"Ladies and gentlemen, let us now delve into the realm of international standards and best practices for digital governance," Emma began, her voice carrying a tone of authority. "As we navigate the complexities of global markets, it's imperative that we adhere to established standards and leverage best practices to guide our governance efforts."

She guided her directors through an exploration of the significance of international standards and best practices, emphasizing the need for alignment with global norms to ensure consistency and effectiveness in governance.

"Our governance practices demand alignment and excellence," Emma continued, her gaze sweeping across the room. "By adhering to internationally recognized standards and adopting best practices, we can demonstrate our commitment to excellence and earn the trust of stakeholders worldwide."

As she spoke, Emma noticed the directors nodding in agreement, their expressions reflecting a shared understanding of the importance of international standards in governance. They recognized that adherence to established norms not only enhanced credibility but also facilitated cross-border collaboration and compliance.

"But international standards and best practices are not static—they evolve in response to changing realities and emerging challenges," Emma added, her tone growing more resolute.

"We must remain vigilant and proactive in staying abreast of developments, continuously refining our governance frameworks to reflect the latest insights and innovations."

She then outlined a strategic approach to international standards and best practices for digital governance, encompassing regular benchmarking against industry peers, participation in global governance forums, and engagement with experts and thought leaders to exchange knowledge and insights.

"As leaders, it's incumbent upon us to lead with diligence and foresight in the pursuit of excellence," Emma declared, her conviction unwavering. "By prioritizing alignment with international standards and best practices, we can elevate our governance efforts to new heights, ensuring our organization's resilience and relevance in an ever-changing world."

As the discussion unfolded, Emma sensed a palpable determination and unity among the directors. The prospect of embracing international standards resonated with them as a collective imperative for ensuring the organization's continued success and leadership in the global marketplace.

"With a commitment to international standards and best practices, we can navigate the complexities of global governance with confidence and integrity," Emma concluded, her voice filled with resolve. "Let's seize this opportunity to lead by example and build a future where our governance practices set the standard for excellence and ethical leadership worldwide."

Collaborative Governance Initiatives at the Global Level

In the prestigious boardroom of GlobalTech Enterprises, Emma Carter redirected the discussion towards a crucial subpoint: collaborative governance initiatives at the global level.

"Ladies and gentlemen, let us now turn our attention to the importance of collaborative governance initiatives at the global level," Emma began, her voice commanding attention. "As we operate in an interconnected world, collaboration with other organizations, industry bodies, and governmental agencies is essential to address shared challenges and drive positive change."

She guided her directors through an exploration of the significance of collaborative governance initiatives, emphasizing the need for collective action to tackle complex issues that transcend organizational and national boundaries.

"Our governance practices demand cooperation and partnership," Emma continued, her eyes scanning the room. "By engaging in collaborative governance initiatives, we can amplify our impact, share best practices, and leverage collective expertise to address global challenges such as climate change, cybersecurity threats, and ethical concerns."

As she spoke, Emma noticed the directors nodding thoughtfully, their expressions reflecting a mix of understanding and anticipation. They recognized that by working together with external stakeholders, they could achieve outcomes that would be unattainable through individual efforts alone.

"But collaborative governance initiatives require more than just participation—they require active engagement, leadership, and a willingness to listen and learn from others," Emma added, her tone growing more resolute. "We must be proactive in seeking out opportunities for collaboration, building trust-based relationships, and fostering a culture of openness and inclusivity."

She then outlined a strategic approach to collaborative

governance initiatives at the global level, encompassing participation in industry associations, partnerships with NGOs and academic institutions, and engagement with international forums and working groups.

"As leaders, it's incumbent upon us to lead with humility and vision in the pursuit of collaborative governance initiatives," Emma declared, her conviction unwavering. "By prioritizing collaboration and partnership, we can harness the collective wisdom and resources of the global community to drive meaningful change and create a better world for future generations."

As the discussion unfolded, Emma sensed a palpable determination and enthusiasm among the directors. The prospect of engaging in collaborative governance initiatives resonated with them as a collective imperative for advancing the organization's mission and values on a global scale.

"With a commitment to collaborative governance initiatives, we can make a significant impact on pressing global issues and demonstrate our commitment to responsible leadership," Emma concluded, her voice filled with resolve. "Let's seize this opportunity to lead by example and build a future where collaboration and partnership are the cornerstones of global governance."

13

Chapter Thirteen; Environmental, Social, and Governance (ESG) in the Digital Age

In the esteemed boardroom of GlobalTech Enterprises, Emma Carter shifted the focus towards a pivotal chapter: Environmental, Social, and Governance (ESG) in the Digital Age.

"Ladies and gentlemen, let us now explore the vital intersection of Environmental, Social, and Governance (ESG) considerations in the Digital Age," Emma began, her voice carrying a tone of urgency. "As stewards of our organization and custodians of our planet, it's imperative that we prioritize sustainability, social responsibility, and ethical governance in all our endeavors."

She guided her directors through an exploration of the significance of ESG considerations, emphasizing the need for holistic decision-making that takes into account the environmental and social impact of business activities alongside traditional governance metrics.

"Our governance practices demand accountability and foresight," Emma continued, her eyes scanning the room. "By integrating ESG principles into our corporate strategy, we can create long-term value for our stakeholders while also contributing to a more sustainable and equitable world."

As she spoke, Emma noticed the directors nodding in agreement, their expressions reflecting a shared understanding of the importance of ESG in driving responsible business practices. They recognized that by aligning with ESG standards, they could enhance their organization's reputation, mitigate risks, and unlock new opportunities for innovation and growth.

"But embracing ESG in the Digital Age requires more than just compliance—it requires leadership, innovation, and a commitment to positive change," Emma added, her tone growing more resolute. "We must leverage technology and data analytics to measure, monitor, and report on our ESG performance transparently, empowering stakeholders to hold us accountable and driving continuous improvement."

She then outlined a comprehensive approach to integrating ESG considerations into corporate governance, encompassing sustainability initiatives, diversity and inclusion programs, and ethical supply chain management practices.

"As leaders, it's incumbent upon us to lead with purpose and integrity in the pursuit of ESG excellence," Emma declared, her conviction unwavering. "By prioritizing Environmental, Social, and Governance considerations, we can build a more resilient and sustainable future for our organization and society as a whole."

As the discussion unfolded, Emma sensed a palpable determination and enthusiasm among the directors. The prospect of embracing ESG principles resonated with them as a collective imperative for driving positive change and leaving a lasting legacy for future generations.

"With a commitment to ESG in the Digital Age, we can create value not only for our organization but for the planet and society as a whole," Emma concluded, her voice filled with resolve. "Let's seize this opportunity to lead by example and build a future where business success is measured not only by financial metrics but by our contributions to a more sustainable and equitable world."

ESG Integration into Digital Strategy

In the hushed ambiance of the GlobalTech Enterprises boardroom, Emma Carter directed the discourse towards a pivotal subpoint: ESG Integration into Digital Strategy.

"Ladies and gentlemen, let us now delve into the critical aspect of integrating Environmental, Social, and Governance (ESG) considerations into our digital strategy," Emma began, her voice resonating with authority. "As we navigate the complexities of the Digital Age, it's imperative that we embed ESG principles into every facet of our digital initiatives, ensuring that sustainability, social responsibility, and ethical governance are at the forefront of our decision-making."

She guided her directors through an exploration of the significance of integrating ESG considerations into digital strategy, emphasizing the need for alignment between organizational goals and societal needs.

"Our digital strategy demands purpose and foresight," Emma continued, her eyes scanning the room. "By weaving ESG considerations into our digital transformation initiatives, we can harness the power of technology to drive positive impact, promote inclusivity, and mitigate environmental risks."

As she spoke, Emma noticed the directors leaning in with heightened interest, their expressions reflecting a mix of understanding and determination. They recognized that by integrating ESG principles into their digital strategy, they could not only enhance their organization's competitive advantage but also contribute to the greater good of society.

"But integrating ESG into our digital strategy is not just about ticking boxes—it's about reimagining how we operate, innovate, and create value in a rapidly evolving landscape," Emma added, her tone growing more resolute. "We must adopt a holistic approach that considers the environmental, social, and governance implications of our digital initiatives from inception to execution, driving meaningful change that benefits both our organization and the world at large."

She then outlined a strategic approach to integrating ESG considerations into digital strategy, encompassing the development of ESG-aligned KPIs, the adoption of sustainable design principles in digital product development, and the implementation of ethical AI frameworks to ensure fairness and transparency in algorithmic decision-making.

"As leaders, it's incumbent upon us to lead with purpose and innovation in the pursuit of ESG integration into digital strategy," Emma declared, her conviction unwavering. "By prioritizing Environmental, Social, and Governance considerations in our digital endeavors, we can pave the way for a more sustainable and equitable future, where technology serves as a force for good and prosperity."

As the discussion unfolded, Emma sensed a palpable determination and enthusiasm among the directors. The prospect of integrating ESG into digital strategy resonated with them as a collective imperative for driving positive change and shaping a future where business success is synonymous with societal impact.

"With a commitment to ESG integration into digital strategy, we can chart a course towards a more sustainable and inclusive Digital Age," Emma concluded, her voice filled with resolve. "Let's seize this opportunity to lead with vision and purpose, and build a future where technology empowers us to create a better world for generations to come."

Leveraging Technology for Sustainable Practices

In the resplendent setting of the GlobalTech Enterprises boardroom, Emma Carter pivoted the discussion towards a pivotal subpoint: Leveraging Technology for Sustainable Practices.

"Ladies and gentlemen, let us now explore the transformative potential of leveraging technology for sustainable practices," Emma began, her voice resonating with purpose. "As we navigate the complexities of the Digital Age, it's imperative that we harness the power of technology to drive innovation, efficiency, and positive environmental impact."

She guided her directors through an exploration of the significance of leveraging technology for sustainable practices, emphasizing the need for technological solutions that promote environmental conservation and resource efficiency.

"Our commitment to sustainability demands innovation and ingenuity," Emma continued, her eyes alight with conviction. "By leveraging technology, we can develop cutting-edge solutions that optimize resource use, reduce carbon emissions, and mitigate environmental risks across our operations and value chain."

As she spoke, Emma noticed the directors nodding in agreement, their expressions reflecting a shared recognition of the transformative potential of technology in driving sustainable practices. They understood that by embracing technological innovations, they could not only enhance their organization's environmental performance but also create value for society and future generations.

"But leveraging technology for sustainable practices is not just about adopting the latest gadgets—it's about reimagining our business processes, supply chains, and product offerings through a sustainability lens," Emma added, her tone growing more resolute. "We must embrace a culture of innovation and collaboration, working hand in hand with partners, suppliers, and stakeholders to co-create solutions that deliver tangible environmental benefits while driving business growth."

She then outlined a strategic approach to leveraging technology for sustainable practices, encompassing initiatives such as renewable energy adoption, IoT-enabled resource management systems, and AI-driven optimization algorithms for supply chain efficiency.

"As leaders, it's incumbent upon us to lead with vision and ambition in the pursuit of sustainable practices through technology," Emma declared, her conviction unwavering. "By prioritizing innovation and collaboration, we can unlock the full potential of technology to address the pressing environmental challenges of our time and build a more sustainable future for all."

As the discussion unfolded, Emma sensed a palpable sense of purpose and excitement among the directors. The prospect of leveraging technology for sustainable practices resonated with them as a collective imperative for driving positive change and shaping a future where technology serves as a catalyst for environmental stewardship and social progress.

"With a commitment to leveraging technology for sustainable practices, we can pioneer new solutions, inspire industry-wide change, and leave a lasting legacy of environmental responsibility," Emma concluded, her voice filled with resolve. "Let's seize this opportunity to lead by example and build a future where sustainability and innovation go hand in hand, creating value for both our organization and the planet."

Measuring and Reporting ESG Performance Digitally

In the luminous confines of the GlobalTech Enterprises boardroom, Emma Carter redirected the conversation towards a pivotal subpoint: Measuring and Reporting ESG Performance Digitally.

"Ladies and gentlemen, let us now delve into the critical aspect of measuring and reporting our Environmental, Social, and Governance (ESG) performance digitally," Emma began, her voice resolute. "As we embark on our journey towards sustainability and responsible governance, it's imperative that we adopt digital tools and methodologies to accurately assess, track, and communicate our progress."

She guided her directors through an exploration of the significance of measuring and reporting ESG performance digitally, emphasizing the need for transparency, accountability, and data-driven decision-making in driving meaningful change.

"Our commitment to ESG demands transparency and integrity," Emma continued, her gaze sweeping across the room.

"By harnessing the power of digital technologies, we can collect, analyze, and visualize data in real-time, providing stakeholders with timely and actionable insights into our environmental, social, and governance performance."

As she spoke, Emma noticed the directors nodding in agreement, their expressions reflecting a shared understanding of the importance of digital measurement and reporting in ESG governance. They recognized that by leveraging digital tools, they could enhance their organization's credibility, strengthen stakeholder trust, and drive continuous improvement in ESG performance.

"But measuring and reporting ESG performance digitally is not just about compliance—it's about driving meaningful change and creating value for our organization and society," Emma added, her tone growing more resolute. "We must embrace a culture of data-driven decision-making, setting ambitious ESG targets, and holding ourselves accountable for achieving them."

She then outlined a strategic approach to measuring and reporting ESG performance digitally, encompassing initiatives such as the implementation of ESG management software, the development of interactive ESG dashboards, and the adoption of blockchain technology for transparent and immutable reporting.

"As leaders, it's incumbent upon us to lead with transparency and innovation in the pursuit of ESG excellence," Emma declared, her conviction unwavering. "By prioritizing digital measurement and reporting, we can demonstrate our commitment to sustainability and responsible governance, driving positive change and creating value for all stakeholders."

As the discussion unfolded, Emma sensed a palpable sense

of purpose and determination among the directors. The prospect of measuring and reporting ESG performance digitally resonated with them as a collective imperative for driving accountability and transparency in their organization's sustainability journey.

"With a commitment to digital measurement and reporting, we can transform our ESG aspirations into tangible outcomes, making a meaningful difference in the world," Emma concluded, her voice filled with resolve. "Let's seize this opportunity to lead by example and build a future where sustainability and responsible governance are at the heart of everything we do."

Investor Expectations and ESG Disclosure Requirements

In the prestigious boardroom of GlobalTech Enterprises, Emma Carter directed the discussion towards a pivotal subpoint: Investor Expectations and ESG Disclosure Requirements.

"Ladies and gentlemen, let us now turn our attention to the critical aspect of investor expectations and ESG disclosure requirements," Emma began, her voice commanding attention. "As we navigate the evolving landscape of responsible investing, it's imperative that we understand and meet the expectations of our investors regarding ESG performance and transparency."

She guided her directors through an exploration of the significance of investor expectations and ESG disclosure requirements, emphasizing the need for proactive engagement and transparent communication with shareholders.

"Our commitment to ESG demands transparency and accountability," Emma continued, her eyes scanning the room. "Investors are increasingly scrutinizing ESG factors when making investment decisions, and they expect companies to disclose relevant information about their environmental, social, and governance practices."

As she spoke, Emma noticed the directors nodding thoughtfully, their expressions reflecting a mix of understanding and determination. They recognized that by aligning with investor expectations and fulfilling ESG disclosure requirements, they could enhance shareholder trust and attract investment capital aligned with their sustainability goals.

"But meeting investor expectations and ESG disclosure requirements is not just about compliance—it's about building trust and credibility with our investors," Emma added, her tone growing more resolute. "We must go beyond mere reporting and engage with investors proactively, demonstrating our commitment to ESG principles and responding to their inquiries and concerns."

She then outlined a strategic approach to meeting investor expectations and ESG disclosure requirements, encompassing initiatives such as regular ESG reporting, participation in ESG ratings and rankings, and engagement with investors through dedicated ESG-focused channels.

"As leaders, it's incumbent upon us to lead with transparency and integrity in our investor relations," Emma declared, her conviction unwavering. "By prioritizing investor expectations and ESG disclosure, we can strengthen our relationships with shareholders, enhance our reputation in the market, and create long-term value for our organization and its stakeholders."

As the discussion unfolded, Emma sensed a palpable sense of purpose and alignment among the directors. The prospect of meeting investor expectations and ESG disclosure requirements resonated with them as a collective imperative for maintaining trust and credibility with the investment community.

"With a commitment to investor expectations and ESG disclosure, we can position ourselves as leaders in responsible investing, attracting capital that aligns with our sustainability goals and driving long-term value creation," Emma concluded, her voice filled with resolve. "Let's seize this opportunity to lead by example and build a future where transparency and accountability are the cornerstones of our investor relations."

Social Impact of Digital Innovations

In the illustrious boardroom of GlobalTech Enterprises, Emma Carter steered the conversation towards a pivotal subpoint: the Social Impact of Digital Innovations.

"Ladies and gentlemen, let us now explore the profound social impact of digital innovations," Emma began, her voice infused with purpose. "As we navigate the Digital Age, it's crucial that we understand and address the implications of our technological advancements on society."

She guided her directors through an exploration of the significance of considering the social impact of digital innovations, emphasizing the need for ethical reflection and responsible decision-making in the development and deployment of new technologies.

"Our commitment to social responsibility demands empathy and foresight," Emma continued, her gaze sweeping across the room. "Digital innovations have the potential to revolutionize industries, improve lives, and drive economic growth, but they also raise complex ethical and societal questions that must be carefully considered."

As she spoke, Emma noticed the directors nodding in agreement, their expressions reflecting a shared recognition of the importance of considering the social implications of their technological endeavors. They understood that by prioritizing social impact alongside technological advancement, they could create a more equitable and inclusive future for all.

"But understanding the social impact of digital innovations is not just about risk mitigation—it's about seizing opportunities to positively influence society," Emma added, her tone growing more resolute. "We must embrace a culture of responsible innovation, ensuring that our digital solutions promote diversity, equity, and inclusion, and empower individuals and communities to thrive in the Digital Age."

She then outlined a strategic approach to addressing the social impact of digital innovations, encompassing initiatives such as stakeholder engagement, impact assessments, and the development of ethical guidelines for technology development and deployment.

"As leaders, it's incumbent upon us to lead with compassion and integrity in our pursuit of technological advancement," Emma declared, her conviction unwavering. "By prioritizing the social impact of digital innovations, we can harness the power of technology to create a more just and sustainable world for future generations."

As the discussion unfolded, Emma sensed a palpable sense of responsibility and determination among the directors. The prospect of considering the social impact of digital innovations resonated with them as a collective imperative for driving positive change and shaping a future where technology serves the greater good.

"With a commitment to addressing the social impact of digital innovations, we can build trust with our stakeholders, foster innovation that benefits society, and leave a lasting legacy of responsible leadership in the Digital Age," Emma concluded, her voice filled with resolve. "Let's seize this opportunity to lead by example and build a future where technology is a force for positive social change."

Case Studies: ESG Leadership in Digital Companies

In the esteemed confines of the GlobalTech Enterprises boardroom, Emma Carter introduced a compelling subpoint: Case Studies of ESG Leadership in Digital Companies.

"Ladies and gentlemen, let us now delve into real-world examples of ESG leadership in digital companies," Emma began, her voice resonating with anticipation. "By examining these case studies, we can glean valuable insights and inspiration for our own journey towards sustainability and responsible governance."

She guided her directors through an exploration of prominent digital companies that had demonstrated exemplary ESG leadership, emphasizing the importance of learning from their successes and challenges.

"Our commitment to ESG demands a willingness to learn and adapt," Emma continued, her eyes alight with enthusiasm. "These case studies offer us a glimpse into the strategies and initiatives that have enabled these companies to excel in environmental, social, and governance performance."

As she spoke, Emma noticed the directors leaning in with keen interest, their expressions reflecting a mix of curiosity and admiration. They understood that by studying the experiences of industry leaders, they could gain valuable insights into best practices and innovative approaches to ESG governance.

"But studying ESG leadership in digital companies is not just about emulation—it's about drawing inspiration and adapting strategies to suit our own unique context and challenges," Emma added, her tone growing more resolute. "We must remain open-minded and creative in our approach, leveraging the lessons learned from these case studies to inform and enhance our own ESG initiatives."

She then proceeded to present a series of case studies, showcasing digital companies that had excelled in various aspects of ESG leadership, from environmental sustainability and social impact to transparent governance and ethical innovation.

"As leaders, it's incumbent upon us to draw wisdom and inspiration from the successes of others," Emma declared, her conviction unwavering. "By studying these case studies of ESG leadership in digital companies, we can chart a course towards greater sustainability, responsibility, and excellence in our own organization."

As the discussion unfolded, Emma sensed a palpable sense of excitement and determination among the directors. The prospect of learning from industry leaders and applying their insights to their own ESG journey resonated with them as a collective imperative for driving continuous improvement and innovation.

"With a commitment to studying and emulating ESG leadership in digital companies, we can accelerate our progress towards sustainability and responsible governance," Emma concluded, her voice filled with optimism. "Let's seize this opportunity to learn, grow, and lead by example in the Digital Age."

14

Chapter Fourteen: Digital Governance and Corporate Reputation Management

In the prestigious boardroom of GlobalTech Enterprises, Emma Carter directed the focus towards a pivotal chapter: Digital Governance and Corporate Reputation Management.

"Ladies and gentlemen, let us now delve into the critical intersection of digital governance and corporate reputation management," Emma began, her voice carrying the weight of significance. "As we navigate the complexities of the Digital Age, safeguarding our corporate reputation has never been more vital."

She guided her directors through an exploration of the importance of digital governance in shaping corporate reputation, emphasizing the need for proactive risk management and strategic communication strategies in the digital realm.

"Our commitment to corporate reputation demands vigilance and resilience," Emma continued, her gaze sweeping across the room. "In the age of social media and instant communication, our reputation can be both our greatest asset and our most vulnerable liability."

As she spoke, Emma noticed the directors nodding in agreement, their expressions reflecting a mix of understanding and determination. They recognized that by prioritizing digital governance and reputation management, they could protect and enhance the organization's brand value and stakeholder trust.

"But safeguarding our corporate reputation is not just about crisis management—it's about fostering a culture of integrity, transparency, and accountability in all our digital interactions," Emma added, her tone growing more resolute. "We must embrace a proactive approach to digital governance, anticipating potential risks and opportunities and responding swiftly and decisively to protect our reputation."

She then outlined a strategic approach to digital governance and corporate reputation management, encompassing initiatives such as social media monitoring, crisis response planning, and stakeholder engagement strategies.

"As leaders, it's incumbent upon us to lead with integrity and foresight in our stewardship of corporate reputation," Emma declared, her conviction unwavering. "By prioritizing digital governance and reputation management, we can build resilience, earn trust, and safeguard our organization's reputation in the Digital Age."

As the discussion unfolded, Emma sensed a palpable sense of urgency and commitment among the directors. The prospect of strengthening digital governance and reputation management resonated with them as a collective imperative for preserving the organization's standing and credibility in an increasingly interconnected world.

"With a commitment to digital governance and reputation management, we can navigate the complexities of the Digital Age with confidence and integrity," Emma concluded, her voice filled with resolve. "Let's seize this opportunity to protect and enhance our corporate reputation, ensuring that we remain a trusted and respected leader in the digital landscape."

Reputation Risks in the Digital Sphere

In the commanding presence of the boardroom at GlobalTech Enterprises, Emma Carter transitioned seamlessly to a pivotal subpoint: Reputation Risks in the Digital Sphere.

"Ladies and gentlemen, let us now confront the formidable challenges posed by reputation risks in the digital sphere," Emma began, her voice commanding attention. "As stewards of our organization's reputation, it's imperative that we acknowledge and address the unique threats presented by the digital landscape."

She guided her directors through an exploration of the intricate web of reputation risks in the digital sphere, emphasizing the need for proactive risk mitigation strategies and swift crisis response mechanisms.

"Our commitment to safeguarding our reputation demands foresight and resilience," Emma continued, her gaze steady and unwavering. "In the digital age, reputation risks can arise from a multitude of sources, including social media controversies, cyberattacks, data breaches, and viral misinformation."

As she spoke, Emma noticed the directors leaning in with rapt attention, their expressions reflecting a mix of concern and determination. They understood that by identifying and understanding reputation risks in the digital sphere, they could better prepare and protect the organization from potential harm.

"But mitigating reputation risks in the digital sphere is not just about reacting to crises—it's about proactive risk management and strategic communication," Emma added, her tone growing more resolute. "We must anticipate potential threats, monitor digital channels vigilantly, and develop robust crisis response plans to protect our reputation in times of adversity."

She then outlined a strategic approach to mitigating reputation risks in the digital sphere, encompassing initiatives such as reputation monitoring tools, cybersecurity measures, employee training programs, and stakeholder communication strategies.

"As leaders, it's incumbent upon us to lead with vigilance and agility in our management of reputation risks," Emma declared, her conviction unwavering. "By prioritizing proactive risk mitigation and swift crisis response in the digital sphere, we can safeguard our organization's reputation and preserve stakeholder trust in the face of evolving threats."

As the discussion unfolded, Emma sensed a palpable sense of resolve and solidarity among the directors. The prospect of confronting reputation risks in the digital sphere resonated with them as a collective imperative for protecting the organization's most valuable asset—its reputation.

"With a commitment to proactive risk management and strategic communication, we can navigate the digital landscape with confidence and resilience," Emma concluded, her voice filled with assurance. "Let's seize this opportunity to fortify our defenses, uphold our reputation, and emerge stronger from any challenge that may arise in the digital sphere."

Monitoring Online Reputation and Sentiment Analysis

In the serene ambiance of the boardroom at GlobalTech Enterprises, Emma Carter shifted the discussion towards a crucial subpoint: Monitoring Online Reputation and Sentiment Analysis.

"Ladies and gentlemen, let us now delve into the indispensable practice of monitoring our online reputation and employing sentiment analysis," Emma began, her tone imbued with gravitas. "In the digital age, the perception of our organization is shaped not only by traditional media but also by the vast and dynamic landscape of online platforms."

She guided her directors through an exploration of the importance of actively monitoring the organization's online reputation and harnessing sentiment analysis tools to gauge public perception accurately.

"Our commitment to safeguarding our reputation demands constant vigilance and insight," Emma continued, her gaze sweeping across the room. "By monitoring online conversations and analyzing sentiment, we can gain valuable insights into how our brand is perceived, identify emerging trends, and detect potential reputational threats before they escalate."

As she spoke, Emma observed the directors nodding in agreement, their expressions reflecting a blend of acknowledgment and determination. They grasped the significance of leveraging technology to stay attuned to public sentiment and proactively manage the organization's reputation in the digital realm.

"But monitoring online reputation and sentiment analysis is not merely about data collection—it's about actionable intelligence and strategic decision-making," Emma emphasized, her voice resolute. "We must interpret the data thoughtfully, discerning meaningful patterns and trends, and leveraging insights to inform our communication strategies and crisis response efforts."

She then outlined a strategic approach to monitoring online reputation and sentiment analysis, detailing initiatives such as social media listening tools, sentiment analysis algorithms, and real-time monitoring dashboards.

"As leaders, it's incumbent upon us to lead with foresight and agility in our management of online reputation," Emma declared, her conviction unwavering. "By prioritizing the monitoring of online reputation and leveraging sentiment analysis, we can proactively safeguard our organization's reputation and maintain stakeholder trust in an ever-evolving digital landscape."

As the discussion unfolded, Emma sensed a palpable sense of determination and commitment among the directors. The prospect of harnessing technology to protect and enhance the organization's reputation resonated with them as a collective imperative for maintaining credibility and resilience in the digital age.

"With a commitment to monitoring online reputation and sentiment analysis, we can navigate the digital landscape with confidence and integrity," Emma concluded, her voice filled with assurance. "Let's seize this opportunity to stay ahead of the curve, anticipate challenges, and preserve our reputation as a trusted leader in the digital realm."

Crisis Communication Strategies I'm the Digital Age

In the commanding presence of the GlobalTech Enterprises boardroom, Emma Carter transitioned seamlessly to a pivotal subpoint: Crisis Communication Strategies in the Digital Age.

"Ladies and gentlemen, let us now address one of the most critical aspects of reputation management: crisis communication strategies in the digital age," Emma began, her voice resolute. "In today's interconnected world, the speed and reach of communication pose both unprecedented challenges and opportunities during times of crisis."

She guided her directors through an exploration of the importance of having robust crisis communication strategies tailored for the digital landscape, emphasizing the need for transparency, authenticity, and agility in responding to crises.

"Our commitment to safeguarding our reputation demands swift and decisive action," Emma continued, her eyes scanning the room. "During times of crisis, the digital realm can amplify the impact of misinformation and rumors, making it imperative that we communicate effectively and transparently to mitigate reputational damage."

As she spoke, Emma noticed the directors nodding in agreement, their expressions reflecting a blend of concern and determination. They understood the urgency of preparing for crises and having clear communication protocols in place to navigate turbulent waters in the digital realm.

"But crisis communication strategies in the digital age are not just about reacting to events—it's about proactive planning and preparation," Emma emphasized, her tone unwavering. "We must anticipate potential crises, develop response protocols, and empower our communication teams to act swiftly and decisively when faced with adversity."

She then outlined a strategic approach to crisis communication in the digital age, detailing initiatives such as crisis response simulations, social media monitoring tools, and stakeholder engagement strategies.

"As leaders, it's incumbent upon us to lead with resilience and transparency in times of crisis," Emma declared, her conviction unyielding. "By prioritizing robust crisis communication strategies, we can mitigate reputational damage, preserve stakeholder trust, and emerge stronger from adversity in the digital age."

As the discussion unfolded, Emma sensed a palpable sense of determination and resolve among the directors. The prospect of preparing for crises and implementing effective communication strategies resonated with them as a collective imperative for safeguarding the organization's reputation and credibility in an unpredictable digital landscape.

"With a commitment to crisis communication strategies in the digital age, we can navigate turbulent waters with confidence and integrity," Emma concluded, her voice filled with assurance. "Let's seize this opportunity to prepare, communicate, and emerge stronger from any challenge that may arise in the digital realm."

Building Trust and Credibility through Transparent Governance

In the commanding atmosphere of the GlobalTech Enterprises boardroom, Emma Carter transitioned seamlessly to a crucial subpoint: Building Trust and Credibility through Transparent Governance.

"Ladies and gentlemen, let us now turn our attention to the cornerstone of reputation management: building trust and credibility through transparent governance," Emma began, her voice imbued with gravitas. "In an era marked by heightened scrutiny and digital transparency, the trust of our stakeholders is paramount to our success."

She guided her directors through an exploration of the significance of transparency in governance, emphasizing its role in fostering trust, enhancing credibility, and mitigating reputational risks in the digital landscape.

"Our commitment to safeguarding our reputation demands unwavering transparency and integrity," Emma continued, her eyes scanning the room. "By embracing transparency in our governance practices, we not only demonstrate accountability to our stakeholders but also strengthen their confidence in our organization's leadership and decision-making processes."

As she spoke, Emma noticed the directors nodding in agreement, their expressions reflecting a mix of acknowledgment and determination. They understood the importance of transparency as a foundational element of responsible governance, especially in an era where information flows freely and accountability is paramount.

"But transparency in governance is not just about disclosure—it's about proactive engagement and meaningful dialogue with our stakeholders," Emma emphasized, her tone unwavering. "We must communicate openly and authentically, soliciting feedback, addressing concerns, and demonstrating our commitment to ethical leadership and corporate responsibility."

She then outlined a strategic approach to fostering transparency in governance, detailing initiatives such as regular reporting, stakeholder forums, ethical guidelines, and whistleblower protection mechanisms.

"As leaders, it's incumbent upon us to lead by example in our commitment to transparent governance," Emma declared, her conviction unyielding. "By prioritizing transparency, we can build trust, enhance credibility, and cultivate enduring relationships with our stakeholders in the digital age."

As the discussion unfolded, Emma sensed a palpable sense of resolve and determination among the directors. The prospect of embracing transparency as a guiding principle of governance resonated with them as a collective imperative for upholding the organization's reputation and integrity in an increasingly transparent and interconnected world.

"With a commitment to transparent governance, we can navigate the complexities of the digital landscape with confidence and integrity," Emma concluded, her voice filled with assurance. "Let's seize this opportunity to build trust, enhance credibility, and demonstrate our unwavering commitment to responsible leadership in the digital age."

Stakeholder Engagement for Reputation Enhancement

In the prestigious boardroom of GlobalTech Enterprises, Emma Carter steered the discussion towards a pivotal subpoint: Stakeholder Engagement for Reputation Enhancement.

"Ladies and gentlemen, let us now explore the transformative power of stakeholder engagement in enhancing our organization's reputation," Emma began, her voice resonating with authority. "In the digital age, our stakeholders wield unprecedented influence, making their engagement essential to our reputation management efforts."

She guided her directors through an exploration of the importance of proactive stakeholder engagement, emphasizing its role in building trust, fostering loyalty, and amplifying positive narratives about the organization.

"Our commitment to safeguarding our reputation demands meaningful and inclusive stakeholder engagement," Emma continued, her eyes scanning the room. "By involving our stakeholders in decision-making processes, listening to their concerns, and responding to their feedback, we demonstrate our dedication to transparency, accountability, and responsible governance."

As she spoke, Emma noticed the directors nodding in agreement, their expressions reflecting a blend of understanding and determination. They recognized the value of cultivating strong relationships with stakeholders as a strategic imperative for reputation enhancement in the digital landscape.

"But stakeholder engagement is not just about communication—it's about collaboration and partnership," Emma emphasized, her tone resolute. "We must foster authentic dialogue, forge mutually beneficial relationships, and co-create value with our stakeholders to drive positive outcomes for our organization and society at large."

She then outlined a strategic approach to stakeholder engagement for reputation enhancement, detailing initiatives such as stakeholder mapping, advisory councils, community partnerships, and corporate social responsibility initiatives.

"As leaders, it's incumbent upon us to lead with empathy and purpose in our stakeholder engagement efforts," Emma declared, her conviction unwavering. "By prioritizing stakeholder engagement, we can amplify our organization's positive impact, strengthen our reputation, and build a legacy of trust and integrity in the digital age."

As the discussion unfolded, Emma sensed a palpable sense of enthusiasm and commitment among the directors. The prospect of engaging stakeholders as partners in reputation enhancement resonated with them as a collective imperative for driving sustainable growth and positive change in the digital era.

"With a commitment to stakeholder engagement, we can harness the collective wisdom and goodwill of our stakeholders to enhance our reputation and achieve our shared goals," Emma concluded, her voice filled with optimism. "Let's seize this opportunity to cultivate meaningful relationships, inspire trust, and leave a lasting legacy of responsible leadership in the digital age."

Digital Marketing and Brand Management in Governance

In the boardroom of GlobalTech Enterprises, Emma Carter steered the discussion towards a critical subpoint: Digital Marketing and Brand Management in Governance.

"Ladies and gentlemen, let us now explore the dynamic realm of digital marketing and its pivotal role in brand management within the realm of governance," Emma began, her voice commanding attention. "In the digital age, our brand is not only shaped by our products and services but also by our online presence and digital interactions."

She guided her directors through an exploration of the importance of strategic digital marketing and brand management, emphasizing its role in shaping perceptions, building loyalty, and enhancing reputation in the digital landscape.

"Our commitment to safeguarding our reputation demands a proactive and strategic approach to digital marketing and brand management," Emma continued, her gaze sweeping across the room. "By leveraging digital channels effectively, we can amplify our brand messaging, engage our audiences, and differentiate ourselves in a crowded marketplace."

As she spoke, Emma noticed the directors nodding in agreement, their expressions reflecting a mix of interest and determination. They understood that in the digital era, a strong and cohesive brand presence was essential for maintaining relevance and credibility.

"But digital marketing and brand management go beyond promotion—they are about storytelling and relationship-building," Emma emphasized, her tone unwavering. "We must craft authentic narratives, resonate with our target audience, and foster meaningful connections that inspire trust and loyalty."

She then outlined a strategic approach to digital marketing and brand management in governance, detailing initiatives such as content marketing strategies, social media engagement plans, online reputation management, and influencer partnerships.

"As leaders, it's incumbent upon us to lead with creativity and authenticity in our digital marketing and brand management efforts," Emma declared, her conviction unwavering. "By prioritizing strategic digital marketing initiatives, we can strengthen our brand presence, enhance our reputation, and create lasting connections with our stakeholders in the digital age."

As the discussion unfolded, Emma sensed a palpable sense of excitement and determination among the directors. The prospect of leveraging digital channels to enhance the organization's brand resonated with them as a collective imperative for staying ahead in a fast-paced and competitive digital landscape.

"With a commitment to strategic digital marketing and brand management, we can elevate our brand presence and amplify our impact in the digital age," Emma concluded, her voice filled with confidence. "Let's seize this opportunity to tell our story, engage our audience, and build a legacy of trust and excellence that transcends the digital realm."

15

Chapter Fifteen: Future Trends and Challenges in Digital Governance

In the esteemed boardroom of GlobalTech Enterprises, Emma Carter led the directors into the final chapter: Future Trends and Challenges in Digital Governance.

"Ladies and gentlemen, as we embark on the final chapter of our journey, let us peer into the future and anticipate the trends and challenges that will shape digital governance," Emma began, her voice projecting a sense of anticipation. "In an era of rapid technological advancement and digital disruption, our ability to adapt and innovate will be paramount to our success."

She guided her directors through an exploration of emerging trends and potential challenges in digital governance, emphasizing the need for foresight, agility, and proactive planning to stay ahead of the curve.

"Our commitment to safeguarding our reputation demands a keen understanding of the evolving digital landscape," Emma continued, her eyes scanning the room. "By anticipating future trends and challenges, we can position ourselves as leaders in digital governance, driving innovation and shaping the future of our organization."

As she spoke, Emma noticed the directors leaning in with keen interest, their expressions reflecting a mix of curiosity and determination. They understood that by staying informed and adaptable, they could navigate the complexities of the digital age with confidence and resilience.

"But the future of digital governance will not be without its challenges," Emma emphasized, her tone unwavering. "From cybersecurity threats and regulatory complexities to ethical dilemmas and technological disruptions, we must be prepared to confront a myriad of challenges head-on."

She then outlined potential future trends and challenges in digital governance, ranging from the adoption of emerging technologies like AI and blockchain to the implications of shifting regulatory landscapes and evolving stakeholder expectations.

"As leaders, it's incumbent upon us to lead with vision and courage in the face of uncertainty," Emma declared, her conviction unyielding. "By embracing change, fostering innovation, and cultivating a culture of continuous learning, we can navigate the future of digital governance with confidence and integrity."

As the discussion unfolded, Emma sensed a palpable sense of anticipation and determination among the directors. The prospect of shaping the future of digital governance resonated with them as a collective imperative for driving sustainable growth and positive change in the digital era.

"With a commitment to foresight and adaptability, we can embrace the future of digital governance as an opportunity for growth and transformation," Emma concluded, her voice filled with optimism. "Let's seize this opportunity to lead with purpose, inspire innovation, and shape a future where digital governance serves as a catalyst for positive change and prosperity."

Anticipating Technological Disruptions and Governance Implications

In the heart of GlobalTech Enterprises' boardroom, Emma Carter transitioned seamlessly to a pivotal subpoint: Anticipating Technological Disruptions and Governance Implications.

"Ladies and gentlemen, as we delve deeper into the future of digital governance, let us turn our attention to the crucial task of anticipating technological disruptions and their governance implications," Emma began, her voice resonating with gravitas. "In an era characterized by rapid innovation and technological advancement, our ability to foresee and adapt to disruptive technologies will be paramount."

She guided her directors through an exploration of emerging technologies and their potential governance implications, emphasizing the need for vigilance, adaptability, and strategic planning to effectively navigate the ever-changing technological landscape.

"Our commitment to safeguarding our reputation demands foresight and proactive planning," Emma continued, her eyes scanning the room. "By identifying emerging technologies and assessing their governance implications, we can position ourselves to capitalize on opportunities and mitigate risks in the digital age."

As she spoke, Emma noticed the directors leaning forward with rapt attention, their expressions reflecting a mix of curiosity and determination. They understood that by staying ahead of technological disruptions, they could steer the organization towards continued success and innovation.

"But technological disruptions bring both opportunities and challenges," Emma emphasized, her tone unwavering. "From the potential of AI and automation to transform business processes, to the ethical dilemmas posed by emerging technologies like facial recognition and biometrics, we must be prepared to confront a range of governance implications."

She then outlined potential technological disruptions and their governance implications, ranging from the impact of AI and automation on workforce dynamics to the ethical considerations surrounding data privacy and algorithmic decision-making.

"As leaders, it's incumbent upon us to lead with vision and adaptability in the face of technological change," Emma declared, her conviction unyielding. "By embracing innovation, fostering a culture of ethical governance, and staying vigilant to emerging trends, we can navigate the future of digital governance with confidence and integrity."

As the discussion unfolded, Emma sensed a palpable sense of anticipation and determination among the directors. The prospect of anticipating technological disruptions and their governance implications resonated with them as a collective imperative for staying ahead in a rapidly evolving digital landscape.

"With a commitment to foresight and strategic planning, we can harness the transformative power of technology to drive positive change and innovation in the digital age," Emma concluded, her voice filled with optimism. "Let's seize this opportunity to lead with purpose, embrace innovation, and shape a future where technology serves as a force for good in governance and beyond."

Shaping the Future of Corporate Governance through Innovation

In the esteemed boardroom of GlobalTech Enterprises, Emma Carter shifted the discussion towards a pivotal subpoint: Shaping the Future of Corporate Governance through Innovation.

"Ladies and gentlemen, as we gaze into the horizon of corporate governance, let us explore the transformative power of innovation in shaping our future," Emma began, her voice resonating with determination. "Innovation is not merely a buzzword; it is the engine driving progress and propelling us towards new frontiers of governance excellence."

She guided her directors through an exploration of how innovation can revolutionize corporate governance, emphasizing the need for bold experimentation, visionary leadership, and a culture of continuous improvement to stay ahead of the curve.

"Our commitment to safeguarding our reputation demands a relentless pursuit of innovation," Emma continued, her eyes locking with each director in turn. "By embracing cutting-edge technologies, reimagining traditional processes, and fostering a spirit of creative thinking, we can redefine the future of corporate governance."

As she spoke, Emma noticed the directors nodding in agreement, their expressions reflecting a mix of anticipation and determination. They understood that in a world of constant change, innovation was not just an option but a necessity for staying relevant and resilient.

"But innovation in corporate governance is not without its challenges," Emma emphasized, her tone unwavering. "From overcoming resistance to change to navigating regulatory complexities, we must be prepared to confront obstacles on our journey towards innovation-driven governance."

She then outlined potential avenues for innovation in corporate governance, ranging from the adoption of AI and blockchain to revolutionize decision-making processes to the implementation of agile governance structures that promote flexibility and adaptability.

"As leaders, it's incumbent upon us to champion innovation as a catalyst for positive change," Emma declared, her conviction unyielding. "By fostering a culture of innovation, empowering our teams to think boldly, and embracing experimentation, we can shape a future of corporate governance that is agile, resilient, and forward-thinking."

As the discussion unfolded, Emma sensed a palpable sense of excitement and determination among the directors. The prospect of shaping the future of corporate governance through innovation resonated with them as a collective imperative for driving sustainable growth and positive change in the digital era.

"With a commitment to innovation, we can unlock new possibilities, drive meaningful progress, and build a legacy of leadership in corporate governance," Emma concluded, her voice filled with optimism. "Let's seize this opportunity to embrace innovation, challenge the status quo, and shape a future where corporate governance sets the standard for excellence and innovation."

Regulatory Outlook for Digital Governance Practices

In the esteemed boardroom of GlobalTech Enterprises, Emma Carter navigated the discussion towards a crucial subpoint: Regulatory Outlook for Digital Governance Practices.

"Ladies and gentlemen, as we chart the course for the future of corporate governance, it is imperative that we examine the regulatory landscape that will shape our journey," Emma began, her voice carrying the weight of authority. "Regulation is the framework within which we operate, and understanding its evolution is essential for navigating the complexities of digital governance."

She guided her directors through an exploration of the regulatory outlook for digital governance practices, emphasizing the need for vigilance, compliance, and proactive engagement with regulatory authorities to ensure alignment with evolving standards.

"Our commitment to safeguarding our reputation demands unwavering compliance with regulatory requirements," Emma continued, her gaze sweeping across the room. "By staying abreast of regulatory developments, anticipating future trends, and engaging constructively with regulators, we can position ourselves as leaders in responsible governance."

As she spoke, Emma noticed the directors leaning in with focused attention, their expressions reflecting a mix of apprehension and resolve. They understood that regulatory compliance was not only a legal obligation but also a strategic imperative for maintaining trust and credibility in the digital age.

"But regulatory compliance is not just about adhering to rules—it's about embracing principles of transparency, accountability, and ethical conduct," Emma emphasized, her tone unwavering. "We must go beyond mere compliance to champion a culture of integrity and responsibility in all our governance practices."

She then outlined the regulatory outlook for digital governance practices, highlighting key areas of focus such as data privacy, cybersecurity, digital ethics, and corporate transparency.

"As leaders, it's incumbent upon us to lead by example in our commitment to regulatory compliance and ethical governance," Emma declared, her conviction unyielding. "By prioritizing compliance, fostering a culture of ethical conduct, and engaging proactively with regulators, we can navigate the regulatory landscape with confidence and integrity."

As the discussion unfolded, Emma sensed a palpable sense of determination and readiness among the directors. The prospect of navigating the regulatory outlook for digital governance resonated with them as a collective imperative for upholding the organization's reputation and integrity in a rapidly evolving regulatory environment.

"With a commitment to regulatory compliance and ethical governance, we can navigate the complexities of the regulatory landscape with confidence and integrity," Emma concluded, her voice filled with assurance. "Let's seize this opportunity to lead by example, embrace regulatory compliance as a strategic advantage, and shape a future where responsible governance sets the standard for excellence and integrity."

Reskilling and Talent Development for Digital Governance Roles

In the prestigious boardroom of GlobalTech Enterprises, Emma Carter transitioned the discussion to a pivotal subpoint: Reskilling and Talent Development for Digital Governance Roles.

"Ladies and gentlemen, as we envision the future of corporate governance, it's essential to recognize the critical role of reskilling and talent development in preparing our workforce for the digital age," Emma began, her voice resonating with purpose. "In an era of rapid technological advancement, our success hinges on the capabilities and competencies of our people."

She guided her directors through an exploration of the importance of reskilling and talent development, emphasizing the need for continuous learning, upskilling, and investment in human capital to thrive in an increasingly digitalized world.

"Our commitment to safeguarding our reputation demands a skilled and adaptable workforce," Emma continued, her eyes locking with each director in turn. "By prioritizing reskilling and talent development initiatives, we can empower our employees to embrace change, drive innovation, and excel in their roles."

As she spoke, Emma noticed the directors nodding in agreement, their expressions reflecting a mix of understanding and determination. They understood that investing in the development of their people was not just a strategic imperative but also a moral obligation to support their professional growth and well-being.

"But reskilling and talent development require more than

just training programs—they demand a culture of continuous learning and a commitment to personal and professional development," Emma emphasized, her tone unwavering. "We must foster an environment where learning is encouraged, knowledge is valued, and growth is celebrated."

She then outlined potential strategies for reskilling and talent development, ranging from investing in digital literacy programs to promoting cross-functional collaboration and providing opportunities for career advancement.

"As leaders, it's incumbent upon us to champion a culture of learning and growth within our organization," Emma declared, her conviction unyielding. "By investing in the reskilling and talent development of our workforce, we can build a team of skilled professionals who are equipped to navigate the complexities of the digital age with confidence and agility."

As the discussion unfolded, Emma sensed a palpable sense of enthusiasm and commitment among the directors. The prospect of investing in the reskilling and talent development of their workforce resonated with them as a collective imperative for driving innovation and staying ahead in a rapidly evolving digital landscape.

"With a commitment to reskilling and talent development, we can empower our workforce to thrive in the digital age and lead our organization to new heights of success," Emma concluded, her voice filled with optimism. "Let's seize this opportunity to invest in our people, unlock their full potential, and shape a future where talent is our greatest asset in the journey of digital governance."

Ethics, Trust, and Accountability in a Hyperconnected World

In the esteemed boardroom of GlobalTech Enterprises, Emma Carter shifted the discussion towards a pivotal subpoint: Ethics, Trust, and Accountability in a Hyperconnected World.

"Ladies and gentlemen, as we navigate the complexities of digital governance, it's imperative that we uphold the highest standards of ethics, trust, and accountability in our actions and decisions," Emma began, her voice carrying the weight of conviction. "In an era of hyperconnectivity, where information travels at the speed of light, our commitment to ethical conduct is more critical than ever."

She guided her directors through an exploration of the importance of ethics, trust, and accountability, emphasizing the need for transparency, integrity, and ethical leadership to foster trust and credibility in an interconnected world.

"Our commitment to safeguarding our reputation demands unwavering adherence to ethical principles," Emma continued, her gaze sweeping across the room. "By prioritizing ethics, trust, and accountability in our governance practices, we can build a foundation of trust with our stakeholders and safeguard our organization's reputation."

As she spoke, Emma noticed the directors nodding in agreement, their expressions reflecting a mix of understanding and determination. They understood that in a world where trust is currency, ethical conduct is not just a moral imperative but also a strategic advantage for building long-term relationships and sustaining business success.

"But maintaining ethics, trust, and accountability requires more than just lip service—it demands a commitment to ethical decision-making, transparent communication, and responsible stewardship," Emma emphasized, her tone unwavering. "We must hold ourselves and each other accountable for upholding the highest standards of conduct in all our interactions."

She then outlined potential strategies for promoting ethics, trust, and accountability, ranging from establishing clear ethical guidelines to implementing robust accountability mechanisms and fostering a culture of transparency and integrity.

"As leaders, it's incumbent upon us to lead by example and set the tone for ethical conduct within our organization," Emma declared, her conviction unyielding. "By prioritizing ethics, trust, and accountability, we can build a culture of integrity that serves as the cornerstone of our governance practices and earns the trust and respect of our stakeholders."

As the discussion unfolded, Emma sensed a palpable sense of determination and commitment among the directors. The prospect of upholding ethics, trust, and accountability in a hyperconnected world resonated with them as a collective imperative for preserving the organization's reputation and integrity in an increasingly transparent and interconnected environment.

"With a commitment to ethics, trust, and accountability, we can navigate the complexities of the hyperconnected world with confidence and integrity," Emma concluded, her voice filled with assurance. "Let's seize this opportunity to lead with integrity, earn the trust of our stakeholders, and shape a future where ethical conduct is the bedrock of our governance practices."

Strategies for Sustaining Effective Digital Governance Over Time

In the boardroom of GlobalTech Enterprises, Emma Carter transitioned the discussion to a pivotal subpoint: Strategies for Sustaining Effective Digital Governance Over Time.

"Ladies and gentlemen, as we embark on our journey towards digital governance excellence, it's crucial that we develop strategies to sustain our progress and effectiveness over time," Emma began, her voice echoing with determination. "In a rapidly evolving landscape, where change is constant, our ability to adapt and evolve will determine our long-term success."

She guided her directors through an exploration of the importance of sustaining effective digital governance, emphasizing the need for agility, resilience, and continuous improvement to navigate the challenges of an ever-changing digital environment.

"Our commitment to safeguarding our reputation demands a steadfast dedication to sustaining our governance practices," Emma continued, her gaze sweeping across the room. "By developing robust strategies for long-term success, we can ensure that our organization remains resilient and adaptive in the face of uncertainty."

As she spoke, Emma noticed the directors nodding in agreement, their expressions reflecting a mix of determination and resolve. They understood that sustaining effective digital governance was not just about achieving short-term goals but also about building a foundation for enduring success and resilience.

"But sustaining effective digital governance requires more

than just reacting to immediate challenges—it demands proactive planning, strategic foresight, and a commitment to continuous improvement," Emma emphasized, her tone unwavering. "We must anticipate future trends, identify emerging risks, and adapt our governance practices accordingly to stay ahead of the curve."

She then outlined potential strategies for sustaining effective digital governance, ranging from investing in innovation and technology to fostering a culture of learning and adaptation and establishing mechanisms for ongoing evaluation and improvement.

"As leaders, it's incumbent upon us to lead with vision and foresight in our commitment to sustaining effective digital governance," Emma declared, her conviction unyielding. "By prioritizing agility, resilience, and continuous improvement, we can position our organization for long-term success and ensure that we remain at the forefront of digital governance excellence."

As the discussion unfolded, Emma sensed a palpable sense of determination and commitment among the directors. The prospect of developing strategies for sustaining effective digital governance resonated with them as a collective imperative for building a resilient and adaptive organization capable of thriving in a rapidly changing digital landscape.

"With a commitment to sustaining effective digital governance, we can navigate the uncertainties of the future with confidence and resilience," Emma concluded, her voice filled with optimism. "Let's seize this opportunity to develop robust strategies, foster a culture of adaptation, and shape a future where our organization remains a leader in digital governance excellence for years to come."

About the Author

Goodson Mumba is a multifaceted individual known for his diverse expertise and prolific contributions across various fields. As an infopreneur, Management Consultant, thought leader, and spiritual leader, he has inspired countless individuals through his insightful teachings and impactful writings. Mumba is also an accomplished author, with several notable works to his name, including "Understanding Corporate Worship," "The Years I Spent in a Week," "Management By Harmony," "The CEO's Diary," "Change to Change" and "Creative Thinking for results" His literary works span topics ranging from business management to personal development and spirituality, reflecting his broad range of interests and insights.

With a Master of Business Leadership (MBL) and a Bachelor of Arts in Theology (BTh), Mumba brings a unique blend of business acumen and spiritual wisdom to his work. His educational background is further enriched by a Group Diploma in Management Studies, providing him with a solid foundation in organizational dynamics and leadership principles. Additionally, Mumba holds diplomas in Education Psychology, Leadership and Management Styles, Organizational Behaviour, Financial Accounting, Economic Growth and Development, and Project Management, showcasing his commitment to continuous learning and professional development.

Mumba's expertise extends beyond traditional academic disciplines, encompassing areas such as Neuro-Linguistic Programming (NLP) and Positive Psychology. His diverse skill set is complemented by a range of certifications, including Creative Problem Solving and Decision Making, Life Coaching Fundamentals and Techniques, Professional Life Coaching, and Performance Management System Design. These certifications reflect Mumba's dedication to equipping himself with the tools and knowledge necessary to empower others and drive positive change.

As an author, Mumba's writings reflect his deep understanding of human nature, organizational dynamics, and spiritual principles. His works offer practical insights, actionable strategies, and inspirational guidance for individuals seeking personal growth, professional success, and spiritual fulfillment. Mumba's holistic approach to life and leadership resonates with readers worldwide, making him a respected figure in both the business and spiritual communities.

Overall, Goodson Mumba's diverse background, extensive knowledge, and profound insights make him a sought-after speaker, mentor, and author. His commitment to excellence, lifelong learning, and service to others continues to inspire individuals to unlock their full potential and lead lives of purpose and significance.

Goodson Mumba is renowned for initiating the concept of Management by Harmony, revolutionizing traditional management practices with a focus on balanced and holistic approaches. He has authored two influential books on this subject: "Introduction to Management by Harmony" and its sequel, "Management by Harmony."

Mumba's work has significantly impacted the field, offering innovative strategies for fostering organizational harmony and efficiency. His contributions continue to shape contemporary management theories and practices.

www.ingramcontent.com/pod-product-compliance
Lightning Source LLC
Chambersburg PA
CBHW052248220526
45471CB00001B/243